Charles Osborne, poet, ~~author~~ ~~and~~ ... ~~assistant~~ istant editor of the *London Ma*... ...g the Arts Council of Great B... ...Director from 1971 until 1986. He was also for some years Director of 'Poetry International', the annual London festival of spoken poetry.

His books include *Kafka, The Complete Operas of Verdi, Wagner and his World, W.H. Auden: The Life of a Poet, Schubert and his Vienna*, and two volumes of poetry, *Swansong* and *Letter to W.H. Auden and Other Poems.*

For automatic updates on your favourite authors visit www.harperperennial.co.uk and register for AuthorTracker.

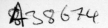

CLASSIC FAVOURITE POEMS

CHOSEN BY
CHARLES OSBORNE

HARPER PERENNIAL
London, New York, Toronto and Sydney

Harper Perennial
An imprint of HarperCollins*Publishers*
77–85 Fulham Palace Road
Hammersmith
London W6 8JB

www.harperperennial.co.uk

This edition published by Harper Perennial 2005
1

First published as *The Collins Book of Best-loved Verse* by Collins in 1986
Published by HarperCollins Publishers in 1992

This selection copyright © Charles Osborne 1986

Charles Osborne asserts the moral right to
be identified as the author of this work

A catalogue record for this book
is available from the British Library

ISBN 0 00 720437 X

Set in Palatino

Printed and bound in Great Britain by
Clays Ltd, St Ives plc

ACKNOWLEDGEMENTS

The publishers gratefully acknowledge permission to reproduce copyright poems in this book.

'Tell Me the Truth About Love' ('Some say that love's a little boy') and 'Lullaby' by W. H. Auden reprinted by permission of Faber and Faber Ltd from *Collected Poems* by W. H. Auden.

'Tarantella' by Hilaire Belloc reprinted by permission of Gerald Duckworth & Co Ltd from *Complete Verse* by Hilaire Belloc.

'A Subaltern's Love-song' and 'Slough' by John Betjeman reprinted by permission of John Murray (Publishers) Ltd from *Collected Poems* by John Betjeman.

'For the Fallen (September 1914)' by Laurence Binyon reprinted by permission of Mrs Nicolete Gray and The Society of Authors on behalf of the Laurence Binyon Estate.

'The Donkey' by G. K. Chesterton reprinted by permission of Miss D. E. Collins from *The Collected Poems of G. K. Chesterton*.

'Leisure' by W. H. Davies reprinted by permission of the Executors of the W. H. Davies Estate and Jonathan Cape Ltd as publishers from *The Complete Poems of W. H. Davies*.

'The Love Song of J. Alfred Prufrock' and 'Journey of the Magi' by T. S. Eliot reprinted by permission of Faber and Faber Ltd from *Collected Poems 1909–1962* by T. S. Eliot.

'Stopping by Woods on a Snowy Evening' and 'The Road Not Taken' by Robert Frost reprinted by permission of the Estate of Robert Frost and Jonathan Cape Ltd as publishers from *The Poetry of Robert Frost* edited by Edward Connery Lathem.

'Time, You Old Gipsy Man' by Ralph Hodgson reprinted by permission of Mrs Ralph Hodgson and Macmillan (London and Basingstoke) from *The Collected Poems of Ralph Hodgson*.

'Loveliest of Trees, the Cherry Now' and 'In Summertime on Bredon' by A. E. Housman reprinted by permission of The Society of Authors as the literary representative of the Estate of A. E. Housman, and Jonathan Cape Ltd, publishers of *Collected Poems* by A. E. Housman.

'If' and 'Boots' by Rudyard Kipling reprinted by permission of The National Trust and Macmillan, London Ltd from *The Definitive Edition of Rudyard Kipling's Verse*.

The Fairies

Up the airy mountain,
  Down the rushy glen,
We daren't go a-hunting
  For fear of little men;
Wee folk, good folk,
  Trooping all together;
Green jacket, red cap,
  And white owl's feather!

Down along the rocky shore
  Some make their home,
They live on crispy pancakes
  Of yellow tide-foam;
Some in the reeds
  Of the black mountain lake,
With frogs for their watch-dogs,
  All night awake.

High on the hill-top
  The old King sits;
He is now so old and gray
  He's nigh lost his wits.
With a bridge of white mist
  Columbkill he crosses,
On his stately journeys
  From Slieveleague to Rosses;
Or going up with music
  On cold starry nights
To sup with the Queen
  Of the gay Northern Lights.

They stole little Bridget
  For seven years long;
When she came down again
  Her friends were all gone.
They took her lightly back,
  Between the night and morrow,
They thought that she was fast asleep,

But she was dead with sorrow.
They have kept her ever since
  Deep within the lake,
On a bed of flag-leaves,
  Watching till she wake.

By the craggy hill-side,
  Through the mosses bare,
They have planted thorn-trees
  For pleasure here and there.
Is any man so daring
  As dig them up in spite,
He shall find their sharpest thorns
  In his bed at night.

Up the airy mountain,
  Down the rushy glen,
We daren't go a-hunting
  For fear of little men;
Wee folk, good folk,
  Trooping all together;
Green jacket, red cap,
  And white owl's feather!

———◦◦———

WILLIAM ALLINGHAM

Dover Beach

The sea is calm to-night.
The tide is full, the moon lies fair
Upon the straits;—on the French coast, the light
Gleams, and is gone; the cliffs of England stand,
Glimmering and vast, out in the tranquil bay.
Come to the window, sweet is the night-air!
Only, from the lone line of spray
Where the sea meets the moon-blanch'd sand,
Listen! you hear the grating roar
Of pebbles which the waves draw back, and fling,
At their return, up the high strand,
Begin, and cease, and then again begin,
With tremulous cadence slow, and bring
The eternal note of sadness in.

Sophocles long ago
Heard it on the Ægæan, and it brought
Into his mind the turbid ebb and flow
Of human misery; we
Find also in the sound a thought,
Hearing it by this distant northern sea.

The Sea of Faith
Was once, too, at the full, and round earth's shore
Lay like the folds of a bright girdle furl'd.
But now I only hear
Its melancholy, long, withdrawing roar,
Retreating, to the breath
Of the night-wind down the vast edges drear
And naked shingles of the world.

Ah, love, let us be true
To one another! for the world, which seems
To lie before us like a land of dreams,
So various, so beautiful, so new,
Hath really neither joy, nor love, nor light,
Nor certitude, nor peace, nor help for pain;
And we are here as on a darkling plain
Swept with confused alarms of struggle and flight,
Where ignorant armies clash by night.

MATTHEW ARNOLD

Tell Me the Truth About Love

Some say that love's a little boy,
  And some say it's a bird,
Some say it makes the world go round,
  And some say that's absurd,
And when I asked the man next-door,
  Who looked as if he knew,
His wife got very cross indeed,
  And said it wouldn't do.

Does it look like a pair of pyjamas,
  Or the ham in a temperance hotel?
Does its odour remind one of llamas,
  Or has it a comforting smell?
Is it prickly to touch as a hedge is,
  Or soft as eiderdown fluff?
Is it sharp or quite smooth at the edges?
  O tell me the truth about love.

Our history books refer to it
  In cryptic little notes,
It's quite a common topic on
  The Transatlantic boats;
I've found the subject mentioned in
  Accounts of suicides,
And even seen it scribbled on
  The backs of railway-guides.

Does it howl like a hungry Alsatian,
  Or boom like a military band?
Could one give a first-rate imitation
  On a saw or a Steinway Grand?
Is its singing at parties a riot?
  Does it only like Classical stuff?
Will it stop when one wants to be quiet?
  O tell me the truth about love.

I looked inside the summer-house;
  It wasn't ever there:
I tried the Thames at Maidenhead,
  And Brighton's bracing air.
I don't know what the blackbird sang,
  Or what the tulip said;
But it wasn't in the chicken-run,
  Or underneath the bed.

Can it pull extraordinary faces?
  Is it usually sick on a swing?
Does it spend all its time at the races,
  Or fiddling with pieces of string?
Has it views of its own about money?
  Does it think Patriotism enough?
Are its stories vulgar but funny?
  O tell me the truth about love.

When it comes, will it come without warning
  Just as I'm picking my nose?
Will it knock on my door in the morning,
  Or tread in the bus on my toes?
Will it come like a change in the weather?
  Will its greeting be courteous or rough?
Will it alter my life altogether?
  O tell me the truth about love.

———•◦•———

W. H. AUDEN

Lullaby

Lay your sleeping head, my love,
Human on my faithless arm;
Time and fevers burn away
Individual beauty from
Thoughtful children, and the grave
Proves the child ephemeral:
But in my arms till break of day
Let the living creature lie,
Mortal, guilty, but to me
The entirely beautiful.

Soul and body have no bounds:
To lovers as they lie upon
Her tolerant enchanted slope
In their ordinary swoon,
Grave the vision Venus sends
Of supernatural sympathy,
Universal love and hope;
While an abstract insight wakes
Among the glaciers and the rocks
The hermit's carnal ecstasy.

Certainty, fidelity
On the stroke of midnight pas
Like vibrations of a bell
And fashionable madmen raise
Their pedantic boring cry:
Every farthing of the cost,
All the dreaded cards foretell,
Shall be paid, but from this night
Not a whisper, not a thought,
Not a kiss nor look be lost.

Beauty, midnight, vision dies:
Let the winds of dawn that blow
Softly round your dreaming head
Such a day of welcome show
Eye and knocking heart may bless,
Find our mortal world enough;
Noons of dryness find you fed
By the involuntary powers,
Nights of insult let you pass
Watched by every human love.

W. H. AUDEN

Tarantella

Do you remember an Inn,
Miranda?
Do you remember an Inn?
And the tedding and the spreading
Of the straw for a bedding,
And the fleas that tease in the High Pyrenees,
And the wine that tasted of the tar?
And the cheers and the jeers of the young muleteers
(Under the vine of the dark verandah)?
Do you remember an Inn, Miranda,
Do you remember an Inn?
And the cheers and the jeers of the young muleteers
Who hadn't got a penny,
And who weren't paying any,
And the hammer at the doors and the Din?
And the Hip! Hop! Hap!
Of the clap
Of the hands to the twirl and the swirl
Of the girl gone chancing,
Glancing,
Dancing,
Backing and advancing,
Snapping of a clapper to the spin
Out and in –
And the Ting, Tong, Tang of the Guitar!
Do you remember an Inn,
Miranda?
Do you remember an Inn?

Never more;
Miranda,
Never more.
Only the high peaks hoar:
And Aragon a torrent at the door.
No sound
In the walls of the Halls where falls
The tread
Of the feet of the dead to the ground
No sound:
But the boom
Of the far Waterfall like Doom.

HILAIRE BELLOC

A Subaltern's Love-song

Miss J. Hunter Dunn, Miss J. Hunter Dunn,
Furnish'd and burnish'd by Aldershot sun,
What strenuous singles we played after tea,
We in the tournament—you against me!

Love-thirty, love-forty, oh! weakness of joy,
The speed of a swallow, the grace of a boy,
With carefullest carelessness, gaily you won,
I am weak from your loveliness, Joan Hunter Dunn.

Miss Joan Hunter Dunn, Miss Joan Hunter Dunn,
How mad I am, sad I am, glad that you won.
The warm-handled racket is back in its press,
But my shock-headed victor, she loves me no less.

Her father's euonymus shines as we walk,
And swing past the summer-house, buried in talk,
And cool the verandah that welcomes us in
To the six-o'clock news and a lime-juice and gin.

The scent of the conifers, sound of the bath,
The view from my bedroom of moss-dappled path,
As I struggle with double-end evening tie,
For we dance at the Golf Club, my victor and I.

On the floor of her bedroom lie blazer and shorts
And the cream-coloured walls are be-trophied with sports,
And westering, questioning settles the sun
On your low-leaded window, Miss Joan Hunter Dunn.

The Hillman is waiting, the light's in the hall,
The pictures of Egypt are bright on the wall,
My sweet, I am standing beside the oak stair
And there on the landing's the light on your hair.

By roads 'not adopted', by woodlanded ways,
She drove to the club in the late summer haze,
Into nine-o'clock Camberley, heavy with bells
And mushroomy, pine-woody, evergreen smells.

Miss Joan Hunter Dunn, Miss Joan Hunter Dunn,
I can hear from the car-park the dance has begun.
Oh! full Surrey twilight! importunate band!
Oh! strongly adorable tennis-girl's hand!

Around us are Rovers and Austins afar,
Above us, the intimate roof of the car,
And here on my right is the girl of my choice,
With the tilt of her nose and the chime of her voice,

And the scent of her wrap, and the words never said,
And the ominous, ominous dancing ahead.
We sat in the car park till twenty to one
And now I'm engaged to Miss Joan Hunter Dunn.

———◦◦———

JOHN BETJEMAN

Slough

Come, friendly bombs, and fall on Slough
It isn't fit for humans now,
There isn't grass to graze a cow
    Swarm over, Death!

Come, bombs, and blow to smithereens
Those air-conditioned, bright canteens,
Tinned fruit, tinned meat, tinned milk, tinned beans
    Tinned minds, tinned breath.

Mess up the mess they call a town—
A house for ninety-seven down
And once a week a half-a-crown
    For twenty years,

And get that man with double chin
Who'll always cheat and always win,
Who washes his repulsive skin
    In women's tears,

And smash his desk of polished oak
And smash his hands so used to stroke
And stop his boring dirty joke
    And make him yell.

But spare the bald young clerks who add
The profits of the stinking cad;
It's not their fault that they are mad,
    They've tasted Hell.

It's not their fault they do not know
The birdsong from the radio,
It's not their fault they often go
    To Maidenhead

And talk of sports and makes of cars
In various bogus Tudor bars
And daren't look up and see the stars
   But belch instead.

In labour-saving homes, with care
Their wives frizz out peroxide hair
And dry it in synthetic air
   And paint their nails.

Come, friendly bombs, and fall on Slough
To get it ready for the plough.
The cabbages are coming now;
   The earth exhales.

———◦•◦———

JOHN BETJEMAN

For the Fallen
(September 1914)

With proud thanksgiving, a mother for her children,
England mourns for her dead across the sea.
Flesh of her flesh they were, spirit of her spirit,
Fallen in the cause of the free.

Solemn the drums thrill: Death august and royal
Sings sorrow up into immortal spheres.
There is music in the midst of desolation
And a glory that shines upon our tears.

They went with songs to the battle, they were young,
Straight of limb, true of eye, steady and aglow.
They were staunch to the end against odds uncounted,
They fell with their faces to the foe.

They shall grow not old, as we that are left grow old:
Age shall not weary them, nor the years condemn.
At the going down of the sun and in the morning
We will remember them.

They mingle not with their laughing comrades again;
They sit no more at familiar tables of home;
They have no lot in our labour of the day-time;
They sleep beyond England's foam.

But where our desires are and our hopes profound,
Felt as a well-spring that is hidden from sight,
To the innermost heart of their own land they are known
As the stars are known to the Night;

As the stars that shall be bright when we are dust,
Moving in marches upon the heavenly plain,
As the stars that are starry in the time of our darkness,
To the end, to the end, they remain.

LAURENCE BINYON

Jerusalem

And did those feet in ancient time
Walk upon England's mountains green?
And was the holy Lamb of God
On England's pleasant pastures seen?

And did the Countenance Divine
Shine forth upon our clouded hills?
And was Jerusalem builded here
Among these dark Satanic Mills?

Bring me my Bow of burning gold!
Bring me my Arrows of desire!
Bring me my Spear! O clouds, unfold!
Bring me my Chariot of fire!

I will not cease from Mental Fight,
Nor shall my Sword sleep in my hand,
Till we have built Jerusalem
In England's green and pleasant land.

WILLIAM BLAKE

A Poison Tree

I was angry with my friend:
I told my wrath, my wrath did end.
I was angry with my foe:
I told it not, my wrath did grow.

And I water'd it in fears,
Night and morning with my tears;
And I sunnèd it with smiles,
And with soft deceitful wiles.

And it grew both day and night,
Till it bore an apple bright;
And my foe beheld it shine,
And he knew that it was mine,

And into my garden stole
When the night had veil'd the pole:
In the morning glad I see
My foe outstretch'd beneath the tree.

WILLIAM BLAKE

The Tiger

Tiger! Tiger! burning bright
In the forests of the night,
What immortal hand or eye
Could frame thy fearful symmetry?

In what distant deeps or skies
Burned the fire of thine eyes?
On what wings dare he aspire?
What the hand dare seize the fire?

And what shoulder, and what art,
Could twist the sinews of thy heart?
And when thy heart began to beat,
What dread hand? And what dread feet?

What the hammer? What the chain?
In what furnace was thy brain?
What the anvil? What dread grasp
Dare its deadly terrors clasp?

When the stars threw down their spears,
And watered heaven with their tears,
Did he smile his work to see?
Did he who made the Lamb make thee?

Tiger! Tiger! burning bright
In the forests of the night,
What immortal hand or eye
Dare frame thy fearful symmetry?

WILLIAM BLAKE

No coward soul is mine

No coward soul is mine
No trembler in the world's storm-troubled sphere:
I see Heaven's glories shine,
And Faith shines equal arming me from Fear.

O God within my breast,
Almighty ever-present Deity!
Life, that in me hast rest,
As I Undying Life, have power in Thee!

Vain are the thousand creeds
That move men's hearts, unutterably vain,
Worthless as withered weeds,
Or idlest froth amid the boundless main,

To waken doubt in one
Holding so fast by thy infinity,
So surely anchored on
The steadfast rock of Immortality.

With wide-embracing love
Thy spirit animates eternal years,
Pervades and broods above,
Changes, sustains, dissolves, creates and rears.

Though Earth and moon were gone,
And suns and universes ceased to be,
And thou wert left alone,
Every Existence would exist in thee.

There is not room for Death
Nor atom that his might could render void:
Since thou art Being and Breath,
And what thou art may never be destroyed.

EMILY BRONTË

23

The Soldier

If I should die, think only this of me:
　That there's some corner of a foreign field
That is for ever England. There shall be
　In that rich earth a richer dust concealed;
A dust whom England bore, shaped, made aware,
　Gave, once, her flowers to love, her ways to roam,
A body of England's, breathing English air,
　Washed by the rivers, blest by suns of home.

And think, this heart, all evil shed away,
　A pulse in the eternal mind, no less
　　Gives somewhere back the thoughts by England given ;
Her sights and sounds ; dreams happy as her day ;
　And laughter, learnt of friends ; and gentleness,
　　In hearts at peace, under an English heaven.

RUPERT BROOKE

from
The Old Vicarage, Grantchester

Ah God! to see the branches stir
Across the moon at Grantchester!
To smell the thrilling-sweet and rotten
Unforgettable, unforgotten
River-smell, and hear the breeze
Sobbing in the little trees.
Say, do the elm-clumps greatly stand
Still guardians of that holy land?
The chestnuts shade, in reverend dream,
The yet unacademic stream?
Is dawn a secret shy and cold
Anadyomene, silver-gold?
And sunset still a golden sea
From Haslingfield to Madingley?

And after, ere the night is born,
Do hares come out about the corn?
Oh, is the water sweet and cool,
Gentle and brown, above the pool?
And laughs the immortal river still
Under the mill, under the mill?
Say, is there Beauty yet to find?
And Certainty? and Quiet kind?
Deep meadows yet, for to forget
The lies, and truths, and pain? . . . oh! yet
Stands the Church clock at ten to three?
And is there honey still for tea?

RUPERT BROOKE

A Musical Instrument

What was he doing, the great god Pan,
  Down in the reeds by the river?
Spreading ruin and scattering ban,
Splashing and paddling with hoofs of a goat,
And breaking the golden lilies afloat
  With the dragon-fly on the river.

He tore out a reed, the great god Pan,
  From the deep cool bed of the river:
The limpid water turbidly ran,
And the broken lilies a-dying lay,
And the dragon-fly had fled away,
  Ere he brought it out of the river.

High on the shore sate the great god Pan,
  While turbidly flowed the river;
And hacked and hewed as a great god can,
With his hard bleak steel at the patient reed,
Till there was not a sign of a leaf indeed
  To prove it fresh from the river.

He cut it short, did the great god Pan
  (How tall it stood in the river!),
Then drew the pith, like the heart of a man,
Steadily from the outside ring,
And notched the poor dry empty thing
  In holes, as he sate by the river.

'This is the way,' laughed the great god Pan
  (Laughed while he sate by the river),
'The only way, since gods began
To make sweet music, they could succeed.'
Then, dropping his mouth to a hole in the reed,
  He blew in power by the river.

Sweet, sweet, sweet, O Pan!
　Piercing sweet by the river!
Blinding sweet, O great god Pan!
The sun on the hill forgot to die,
And the lilies revived, and the dragon-fly
　Came back to dream on the river.

Yet half a beast is the great god Pan,
　To laugh as he sits by the river,
Making a poet out of a man:
The true gods sigh for the cost and pain, –
For the reed which grows nevermore again
　As a reed with the reeds in the river.

———◆◇◆———

ELIZABETH BARRETT BROWNING

Sonnet 43 from
Sonnets from the Portuguese

How do I love thee? Let me count the ways.
I love thee to the depth and breadth and height
My soul can reach, when feeling out of sight
For the ends of Being and ideal Grace.
I love thee to the level of everyday's
Most quiet need, by sun and candle-light.
I love thee freely, as men strive for Right;
I love thee purely, as they turn from Praise.
I love thee with the passion put to use
In my old griefs, and with my childhood's faith.
I love thee with a love I seemed to lose
With my lost saints, – I love thee with the breath,
Smiles, tears, of all my life! – and, if God choose,
I shall but love thee better after death.

ELIZABETH BARRETT BROWNING

Home Thoughts from Abroad

Oh, to be in England
Now that April's there,
And whoever wakes in England
Sees, some morning, unaware,
That the lowest boughs and the brushwood sheaf
Round the elm-tree bole are in tiny leaf,
While the chaffinch sings on the orchard bough
In England – now!
And after April, when May follows,
And the whitethroat builds, and all the swallows!
Hark, where my blossomed pear-tree in the hedge
Leans to the field and scatters on the clover
Blossoms and dewdrops – at the bent spray's edge –
That's the wise thrush; he sings each song twice over,
Lest you should think he never could recapture
The first fine careless rapture!
And though the fields look rough with hoary dew
All will be gay when noontide wakes anew
The buttercups, the little children's dower
– Far brighter than this gaudy melon-flower!

ROBERT BROWNING

Home Thoughts from the Sea

Nobly, nobly Cape Saint Vincent to the North-west died away;
Sunset ran, one glorious blood-red, reeking into Cadiz Bay;
Bluish 'mid the burning water, full in face Trafalgar lay;
In the dimmest North-east distance dawned Gibraltar grand and
    gray ;
'Here and here did England help me: how can I help England?' –
    say,
Whoso turns as I, this evening, turn to God to praise and pray.
While Jove's planet rises yonder, silent over Africa.

ROBERT BROWNING

My Last Duchess

That's my last Duchess painted on the wall,
Looking as if she were alive. I call
That piece a wonder, now: Frà Pandolf's hands
Worked busily a day, and there she stands.
Will 't please you sit and look at her? I said
'Frà Pandolf' by design, for never read
Strangers like you that pictured countenance,
The depth and passion of its earnest glance,
But to myself they turned (since none puts by
The curtain I have drawn for you, but I)
And seemed as they would ask me, if they durst,
How such a glance came there; so, not the first
Are you to turn and ask thus. Sir, 't was not
Her husband's presence only, called that spot
Of joy into the Duchess' cheek: perhaps
Frà Pandolf chanced to say 'Her mantle laps
Over my lady's wrist too much,' or 'Paint
Must never hope to reproduce the faint
Half-flush that dies along her throat:' such stuff
Was courtesy, she thought, and cause enough
For calling up that spot of joy. She had
A heart – how shall I say? – too soon made glad,
Too easily impressed; she liked whate'er
She looked on, and her looks went everywhere.
Sir, 't was all one! My favour at her breast,
The dropping of the daylight in the West,
The bough of cherries some officious fool
Broke in the orchard for her, the white mule
She rode with round the terrace – all and each
Would draw from her alike the approving speech,
Or blush, at least. She thanked men, – good! but thanked
Somehow – I know not how – as if she ranked
My gift of a nine-hundred-years-old name
With anybody's gift. Who'd stoop to blame
This sort of trifling? Even had you skill
In speech – (which I have not) – to make your will
Quite clear to such an one, and say, 'Just this
Or that in you disgusts me; here you miss,

Or there exceed the mark' – and if she let
Herself be lessoned so, nor plainly set
Her wits to yours, forsooth, and made excuse,
– E'en then would be some stooping; and I choose
Never to stoop. Oh sir, she smiled, no doubt,
Whene'er I passed her; but who passed without
Much the same smile? This grew; I gave commands;
Then all smiles stopped together. There she stands
As if alive. Will 't please you rise? We'll meet
The company below, then. I repeat,
The Count your master's known munificence
Is ample warrant that no just pretence
Of mine for dowry will be disallowed;
Though his fair daughter's self, as I avowed
At starting, is my object. Nay, we'll go
Together down, sir. Notice Neptune, though,
Taming a sea-horse, thought a rarity,
Which Claus of Innsbruck cast in bronze for me!

———•◦•———

ROBERT BROWNING

32

How They Brought the Good News from Ghent to Aix

I sprang to the stirrup, and Joris, and he;
I galloped, Dirck galloped, we galloped all three;
'Good speed!' cried the watch, as the gate-bolts undrew;
'Speed!' echoed the wall to us galloping through;
Behind shut the postern, the lights sank to rest,
And into the midnight we galloped abreast.

Not a word to each other: we kept the great pace
Neck by neck, stride by stride, never changing our place;
I turned in my saddle and made its girths tight,
Then shortened each stirrup, and set the pique right,
Rebuckled the cheek-strap, chained slacker the bit,
Nor galloped less steadily Roland a whit.

'Twas moonset at starting; but while we drew near
Lokeren, the cocks crew and twilight dawned clear;
At Boom, a great yellow star came out to see;
At Düffeld, 'twas morning as plain as could be;
And from Mecheln church-steeple we heard the half-chime,
So Joris broke silence with, 'Yet there is time!'

At Aerschot, up leaped of a sudden the sun,
And against him the cattle stood black every one,
To stare thro' the mist at us galloping past,
And I saw my stout galloper Roland at last,
With resolute shoulders, each butting away
The haze, as some bluff river headland its spray.

And his low head and crest, just one sharp ear bent back
For my voice, and the other pricked out on his track;
And one eye's black intelligence, – ever that glance
O'er its white edge at me, his own master, askance!
And the thick heavy spume-flakes which aye and anon
His fierce lips shook upwards in galloping on.

By Hasselt, Dirck groaned; and cried Joris, 'Stay spur!
Your Roos galloped bravely, the fault's not in her,
We'll remember at Aix' – for one heard the quick wheeze
Of her chest, saw the stretched neck and staggering knees,
And sunk tail, and horrible heave of the flank,
As down on her haunches she shuddered and sank.

So we were left galloping, Joris and I,
Past Looz and past Tongres, no cloud in the sky;
The broad sun above laughed a pitiless laugh,
'Neath our feet broke the brittle bright stubble like chaff;
Till over by Dalhem a dome-spire sprang white,
And 'Gallop,' gasped Joris, 'for Aix is in sight!'

'How they'll greet us!' – and all in a moment his roan
Rolled neck and croup over, lay dead as a stone;
And there was my Roland to bear the whole weight
Of the news which alone could save Aix from her fate,
With his nostrils like pits full of blood to the brim,
And with circles of red for his eye-sockets' rim.

Then I cast loose my buffcoat, each holster let fall,
Shook off both my jack-boots, let go belt and all,
Stood up in the stirrup, leaned, patted his ear,
Called my Roland his pet-name, my horse without peer;
Clapped my hands, laughed and sang, any noise, bad or good,
Till at length into Aix Roland galloped and stood.

And all I remember is, friends flocking round
As I sat with his head 'twixt my knees on the ground ;
And no voice but was praising this Roland of mine,
As I poured down his throat our last measure of wine,
Which (the burgesses voted by common consent)
Was no more than his due who brought good news from Ghent.

———◦◦———

ROBERT BROWNING

The Shepherd Boy Sings in the Valley of Humiliation

He that is down needs fear no fall,
  He that is low, no pride;
He that is humble ever shall
  Have God to be his guide.

I am content with what I have,
  Little be it or much:
And, Lord, contentment still I crave,
  Because Thou savest such.

Fullness to such a burden is
  That go on pilgrimage:
Here little, and hereafter bliss,
  Is best from age to age.

JOHN BUNYAN

The Banks o' Doon

Ye banks and braes o' bonnie Doon,
  How can ye bloom sae fresh and fair?
How can ye chant, ye little birds,
  And I sae weary fu' o' care?
Thou'lt break my heart, thou warbling bird,
  That wantons thro' the flowering thorn:
Thou minds me o' departed joys,
  Departed never to return.

Aft hae I roved by bonnie Doon,
  To see the rose and woodbine twine;
And ilka bird sang o' its love,
  And fondly sae did I o' mine.
Wi' lightsome heart I pu'd a rose,
  Fu' sweet upon its thorny tree;
And my fause lover stole my rose,
  But ah! he left the thorn wi' me.

ROBERT BURNS

A Red, Red Rose

O, my luve's like a red, red rose,
  That's newly sprung in June;
O, my luve's like the melodie
  That's sweetly play'd in tune.

As fair art thou, my bonnie lass,
  So deep in luve am I;
And I will luve thee still, my dear,
  Till a' the seas gang dry –

Till a' the seas gang dry, my dear,
  And the rocks melt wi' the sun;
I will luve thee still, my dear,
  While the sands of life shall run.

And fare thee weel, my only luve!
  And fare thee weel a while!
And I will come again, my luve,
  Tho' it were ten thousand mile.

ROBERT BURNS

My Heart's in the Highlands

My heart's in the Highlands, my heart is not here;
My heart's in the Highlands a-chasing the deer;
Chasing the wild deer, and following the roe,
My heart's in the Highlands wherever I go.
Farewell to the Highlands, farewell to the North,
The birth-place of valour, the country of worth;
Wherever I wander, wherever I rove,
The hills of the Highlands for ever I love.
Farewell to the mountains high cover'd with snow;
Farewell to the straths and green valleys below;
Farewell to the forests and wild-hanging woods;
Farewell to the torrents and loud-pouring floods.
My heart's in the Highlands, my heart is not here,
My heart's in the Highlands a-chasing the deer;
Chasing the wild deer, and following the roe,
My heart's in the Highlands, wherever I go.

ROBERT BURNS

She Walks in Beauty

She walks in beauty, like the night
Of cloudless climes and starry skies,
And all that's best of dark and bright
Meets in her aspect and her eyes,
Thus mellow'd to that tender light
Which heaven to gaudy day denies.

One shade the more, one ray the less
Had half impair'd the nameless grace
Which waves in every raven tress
Or softly lightens o'er her face,
Where thoughts serenely sweet express
How pure, how dear their dwelling-place.

And on that cheek and o'er that brow
So soft, so calm, yet eloquent,
The smiles that win, the tints that glow
But tell of days in goodness spent, –
A mind at peace with all below,
A heart whose love is innocent.

LORD BYRON

So, We'll Go No More a-Roving

So, we'll go no more a-roving
    So late into the night,
Though the heart be still as loving,
    And the moon be still as bright.

For the sword outwears its sheath,
    And the soul wears out the breast,
And the heart must pause to breathe,
    And love itself have rest.

Though the night was made for loving,
    And the day returns too soon,
Yet we'll go no more a-roving
    By the light of the moon.

LORD BYRON

The Destruction of Sennacherib

The Assyrian came down like the wolf on the fold,
And his cohorts were gleaming in purple and gold;
And the sheen of their spears was like stars on the sea,
When the blue wave rolls nightly on deep Galilee.

Like the leaves of the forest when Summer is green,
That host with their banners at sunset were seen:
Like the leaves of the forest when Autumn hath blown,
That host on the morrow lay withered and strown.

For the Angel of Death spread his wings on the blast,
And breathed in the face of the foe as he passed;
And the eyes of the sleepers waxed deadly and chill,
And their hearts but once heaved, and for ever grew still!

And there lay the steed with his nostril all wide,
But through it there rolled not the breath of his pride:
And the foam of his gasping lay white on the turf,
And cold as the spray of the rock-beating surf.

And there lay the rider distorted and pale,
With the dew on his brow and the rust on his mail;
And the tents were all silent, the banners alone,
The lances unlifted, the trumpet unblown.

And the widows of Ashur are loud in their wail,
And the idols are broke in the temple of Baal;
And the might of the Gentile, unsmote by the sword,
Hath melted like snow in the glance of the Lord!

LORD BYRON

Ye Mariners of England

Ye Mariners of England
  That guard our native seas!
Whose flag has braved a thousand years
  The battle and the breeze!
Your glorious standard launch again
  To match another foe;
And sweep through the deep,
  While the stormy winds do blow!
While the battle rages loud and long
  And the stormy winds do blow.

The spirits of your fathers
  Shall start from every wave –
For the deck it was their field of fame,
  And Ocean was their grave:
Where Blake and mighty Nelson fell
  Your manly hearts shall glow,
As ye sweep through the deep,
  While the stormy winds do blow!
While the battle rages loud and long
  And the stormy winds do blow.

Britannia needs no bulwarks,
  No towers along the steep;
Her march is o'er the mountain-waves,
  Her home is on the deep.
With thunders from her native oak
  She quells the floods below,
As they roar on the shore,
  When the stormy winds do blow!
When the battle rages loud and long,
  And the stormy winds do blow.

The meteor flag of England
  Shall yet terrific burn;
Till danger's troubled night depart
  And the star of peace return.
Then, then, ye ocean-warriors!
  Our song and feast shall flow
To the fame of your name,
  When the storm has ceased to blow!
When the fiery fight is heard no more,
  And the storm has ceased to blow.

———◆◇◆———

THOMAS CAMPBELL

Lord Ullin's Daughter

A chieftain to the Highlands bound
Cries 'Boatman, do not tarry!
And I'll give thee a silver pound
To row us o'er the ferry!'

'Now who be ye, would cross Lochgyle
This dark and stormy water?'
'O I'm the chief of Ulva's isle,
And this, Lord Ullin's daughter.

'And fast before her father's men
Three days we've fled together,
For should he find us in the glen,
My blood would stain the heather.

'His horsemen hard behind us ride –
Should they our steps discover,
Then who will cheer my bonny bride
When they have slain her lover?'

Out spoke the hardy Highland wight,
'I'll go, my chief, I'm ready:
It is not for your silver bright,
But for your winsome lady: –

'And by my word! the bonny bird
In danger shall not tarry;
So though the waves are raging white
I'll row you o'er the ferry.'

By this the storm grew loud apace,
The water-wraith was shrieking;
And in the scowl of heaven each face
Grew dark as they were speaking.

But still as wilder blew the wind
And as the night grew drearer,
Adown the glen rode armèd men,
Their trampling sounded nearer.

'O haste thee, haste!' the lady cries,
'Though tempests round us gather;
I'll meet the raging of the skies,
But not an angry father.'

The boat has left a stormy land,
A stormy sea before her, –
When, O! too strong for human hand
The tempest gather'd o'er her.

And still they row'd amidst the roar
Of waters fast prevailing:
Lord Ullin reach'd that fatal shore, –
His wrath was changed to wailing.

For, sore dismay'd, through storm and shade
His child he did discover: –
One lovely hand she stretch'd for aid,
And one was round her lover.

'Come back! come back!' he cried in grief
'Across this stormy water:
And I'll forgive your Highland chief,
My daughter! – O my daughter!'

'Twas vain: the loud waves lash'd the shore,
Return or aid preventing:
The waters wild went o'er his child,
And he was left lamenting.

———◦◦———

THOMAS CAMPBELL

Sally in our Alley

Of all the girls that are so smart
 There's none like pretty Sally;
She is the darling of my heart,
 And she lives in our alley.
There is no lady in the land
 Is half so sweet as Sally;
She is the darling of my heart,
 And she lives in our alley.

Her father he makes cabbage-nets
 And through the streets does cry 'em;
Her mother she sells laces long
 To such as please to buy 'em:
But sure such folks could ne'er beget
 So sweet a girl as Sally!
She is the darling of my heart,
 And she lives in our alley.

When she is by, I leave my work,
 I love her so sincerely;
My master comes like any Turk,
 And bangs me most severely –
But let him bang his bellyful,
 I'll bear it all for Sally;
She is the darling of my heart,
 And she lives in our alley.

Of all the days that's in the week
 I dearly love but one day –
And that's the day that comes betwixt
 A Saturday and Monday;
For then I'm drest all in my best
 To walk abroad with Sally;
She is the darling of my heart,
 And she lives in our alley.

My master carries me to church,
   And often am I blamed
Because I leave him in the lurch
   As soon as text is named;
I leave the church in sermon-time
   And slink away to Sally;
She is the darling of my heart,
   And she lives in our alley.

When Christmas comes about again
   O then I shall have money;
I'll hoard it up, and box it all,
   I'll give it to my honey:
I would it were ten thousand pound,
   I'd give it all to Sally;
She is the darling of my heart,
   And she lives in our alley.

My master and the neighbours all
   Make game of me and Sally,
And, but for her, I'd better be
   A slave and row a galley;
But when my seven long years are out
   O then I'll marry Sally, –
O then we'll wed, and then we'll bed,
   But not in our alley!

—◆◇◆—

HENRY CAREY

Jabberwocky

'Twas brillig, and the slithy toves
  Did gyre and gimble in the wabe;
All mimsy were the borogoves,
  And the mome raths outgrabe.

'Beware the Jabberwock, my son!
  The jaws that bite, the claws that catch!
Beware the Jubjub bird, and shun
  The frumious Bandersnatch!'

He took his vorpal sword in hand:
  Long time the manxome foe he sought –
So rested he by the Tumtum tree,
  And stood awhile in thought.

And as in uffish thought he stood,
  The Jabberwock, with eyes of flame,
Came whiffling through the tulgey wood,
  And burbled as it came!

One, two! One, two! And through and through
  The vorpal blade went snicker-snack!
He left it dead, and with its head
  He went galumphing back.

'And hast thou slain the Jabberwock!
  Come to my arms, my beamish boy!
O frabjous day! Callooh! Callay!'
  He chortled in his joy.

'Twas brillig, and the slithy toves
  Did gyre and gimble in the wabe;
All mimsy were the borogoves,
  And the mome raths outgrabe.

LEWIS CARROLL

The Donkey

When fishes flew and forests walked
  And figs grew upon thorn,
Some moment when the moon was blood
  Then surely I was born.

With monstrous head and sickening cry
  And ears like errant wings,
The devil's walking parody
  On all four-footed things.

The tattered outlaw of the earth,
  Of ancient crooked will;
Starve, scourge, deride me: I am dumb,
  I keep my secret still.

Fools! For I also had my hour;
  One far fierce hour and sweet:
There was a shout about my ears,
  And palms before my feet.

G. K. CHESTERTON

Say not the Struggle Nought Availeth

Say not the struggle nought availeth,
   The labour and the wounds are vain,
The enemy faints not, nor faileth,
   And as things have been, things remain.

If hopes were dupes, fears may be liars;
   It may be, in yon smoke concealed,
Your comrades chase e'en now the fliers,
   And, but for you, possess the field.

For while the tired waves, vainly breaking,
   Seem here no painful inch to gain,
Far back through creeks and inlets making
   Came, silent, flooding in, the main,

And not by eastern windows only,
   When daylight comes, comes in the light,
In front the sun climbs slow, how slowly,
   But westward, look, the land is bright.

ARTHUR HUGH CLOUGH

Kubla Khan

In Xanadu did Kubla Khan
A stately pleasure-dome decree:
Where Alph, the sacred river, ran
Through caverns measureless to man
  Down to a sunless sea.
So twice five miles of fertile ground
With walls and towers were girdled round:
And there were gardens bright with sinuous rills,
Where blossomed many an incense-bearing tree,
And here were forests ancient as the hills,
Enfolding sunny spots of greenery.

But oh! that deep romantic chasm which slanted
Down the green hill athwart a cedarn cover!
A savage place! as holy and enchanted
As e'er beneath a waning moon was haunted
By woman wailing for her demon-lover!

And from this chasm, with ceaseless turmoil seething,
As if this earth in fast thick pants were breathing,
A mighty fountain momently was forced:
Amid whose swift half-intermitted burst
Huge fragments vaulted like rebounding hail,
Or chaffy grain beneath the thresher's flail:
And 'mid these dancing rocks at once and ever
It flung up momently the sacred river.
Five miles meandering with a mazy motion
Through wood and dale the sacred river ran,
Then reached the caverns measureless to man,
And sank in tumult to a lifeless ocean:
And 'mid this tumult Kubla heard from far
Ancestral voices prophesying war!

The shadow of the dome of pleasure
Floated midway on the waves;
Where was heard the mingled measure
From the fountain and the caves.
It was a miracle of rare device,
A sunny pleasure-dome with caves of ice!

A damsel with a dulcimer
In a vision once I saw:
It was an Abyssinian maid,
And on her dulcimer she played,
Singing of Mount Abora.
Could I revive within me
Her symphony and song,
To such a deep delight 'twould win me,
That with music loud and long,
I would build that dome in air,
That sunny dome! those caves of ice!
And all who heard should see them there,
And all should cry, Beware! Beware!
His flashing eyes, his floating hair!
Weave a circle round him thrice,
And close your eyes with holy dread,
For he on honey-dew hath fed,
And drunk the milk of Paradise.

———◦◦———

SAMUEL TAYLOR COLERIDGE

Heraclitus

They told me, Heraclitus, they told me you were dead;
They brought me bitter news to hear and bitter tears to shed.
I wept, as I remembered, how often you and I
Had tired the sun with talking and sent him down the sky.

And now that thou art lying, my dear old Carian guest,
A handful of grey ashes, long long ago at rest,
Still are thy pleasant voices, thy nightingales, awake,
For Death, he taketh all away, but them he cannot take.

WILLIAM JOHNSON CORY

Verses Supposed to be Written by Alexander Selkirk

I am monarch of all I survey;
My right there is none to dispute;
From the centre all round to the sea
I am lord of the fowl and the brute.
O Solitude! where are the charms
That sages have seen in thy face?
Better dwell in the midst of alarms
Than reign in this horrible place.

I am out of humanity's reach,
I must finish my journey alone,
Never hear the sweet music of speech;
I start at the sound of my own.
The beasts that roam over the plain
My form with indifference see;
They are so unacquainted with man,
Their tameness is shocking to me.

Society, Friendship, and Love
Divinely bestow'd upon man,
O had I the wings of a dove
How soon would I taste you again!
My sorrows I then might assuage
In the ways of religion and truth,
Might learn from the wisdom of age,
And be cheer'd by the sallies of youth.

Ye winds that have made me your sport,
Convey to this desolate shore
Some cordial endearing report
Of a land I shall visit no more:
My friends, do they now and then send
A wish or a thought after me?
O tell me I yet have a friend,
Though a friend I am never to see.

How fleet is a glance of the mind!
Compared with the speed of its flight,
The tempest itself lags behind,
And the swift-wingèd arrows of light.
When I think of my own native land
In a moment I seem to be there;
But alas! recollection at hand
Soon hurries me back to despair.

But the seafowl is gone to her nest,
The beast is laid down in his lair;
Even here is a season of rest,
And I to my cabin repair.
There's mercy in every place,
And mercy, encouraging thought!
Gives even affliction a grace
And reconciles man to his lot.

———◦◦◦———

WILLIAM COWPER

A Wet Sheet and a Flowing Sea

A wet sheet and a flowing sea,
  A wind that follows fast
And fills the white and rustling sail
  And bends the gallant mast;
And bends the gallant mast, my boys,
  While like the eagle free
Away the good ship flies and leaves
  Old England on the lee.

O for a soft and gentle wind!
  I heard a fair one cry;
But give to me the snoring breeze
  And white waves heaving high;
And white waves heaving high, my lads,
  The good ship tight and free –
The world of waters is our home,
  And merry men are we.

There's tempest in yon hornèd moon,
  And lightning in yon cloud;
But hark the music, mariners!
  The wind is piping loud;
The wind is piping loud, my boys,
  The lightning flashes free –
While the hollow oak our palace is,
  Our heritage the sea.

ALLAN CUNNINGHAM

Leisure

What is this life if, full of care,
We have no time to stand and stare.

No time to stand beneath the boughs
And stare as long as sheep or cows.

No time to see, when woods we pass,
Where squirrels hide their nuts in grass.

No time to see, in broad daylight,
Streams full of stars like skies at night.

No time to turn at Beauty's glance,
And watch her feet, how they can dance.

No time to wait till her mouth can
Enrich that smile her eyes began.

A poor life this if, full of care,
We have no time to stand and stare.

W. H. DAVIES

Parting

My life closed twice before its close –
It yet remains to see
If Immortality unveil
A third event to me

So huge, so hopeless to conceive
As these that twice befell.
Parting is all we know of heaven,
And all we need of hell.

Emily Dickinson

The Sun Rising

Busy old fool, unruly Sun,
Why dost thou thus,
Through windows and through curtains call on us?
Must to thy motions lovers' seasons run?
Saucy pedantic wretch, go chide
Late school-boys, and sour 'prentices,
Go tell court-huntsmen that the King will ride,
Call country ants to harvest offices;
Love, all alike, no season knows, nor clime,
Nor hours, days, months, which are the rags of time.

Thy beams, so reverend and strong
Why shouldst thou think?
I could eclipse and cloud them with a wink,
But that I would not lose her sight so long:
If her eyes have not blinded thine,
Look, and tomorrow late tell me,
Whether both the Indias of spice and mine
Be where thou left'st them, or lie here with me.
Ask for those kings whom thou saw'st yesterday,
And thou shalt hear, 'All here in one bed lay.'

She's all States, and all Princes I;
Nothing else is.
Princes do but play us; compared to this,
All honour's mimic; all wealth alchemy.
Thou, Sun, art half as happy as we,
In that the world's contracted thus;
Thine age asks ease, and since thy duties be
To warm the world, that's done in warming us.
Shine here to us, and thou art everywhere ;
This bed thy centre is, these walls thy sphere.

JOHN DONNE

Death, Be Not Proud

Death, be not proud, though some have callèd thee
Mighty and dreadful, for thou art not so:
For those whom thou think'st thou dost overthrow
Die not, poor Death; nor yet canst thou kill me.
From Rest and Sleep, which but thy pictures be,
Much pleasure, then from thee much more must flow;
And soonest our best men with thee do go –
Rest of their bones and souls' delivery.
Thou'rt slave to fate, chance, kings, and desperate men,
And dost with poison, war, and sickness dwell;
And poppy or charms can make us sleep as well
And better than thy stroke. Why swell'st thou then?
One short sleep past, we wake eternally,
And Death shall be no more: Death, thou shalt die.

JOHN DONNE

The Love Song of J. Alfred Prufrock

*S'io credessi che mia risposta fosse
a persona che mai tornasse al mondo,
questa fiamma staria senza più scosse.
Ma per ciò che giammai di questo fondo
non tornò vivo alcun, s'i'odo il vero,
senza tema d'infamia ti rispondo.*

Let us go then, you and I,
When the evening is spread out against the sky
Like a patient etherised upon a table;
Let us go, through certain half-deserted streets,
The muttering retreats
Of restless nights in one-night cheap hotels
And sawdust restaurants with oyster-shells:
Streets that follow like a tedious argument
Of insidious intent
To lead you to an overwhelming question . . .
Oh, do not ask, 'What is it?'
Let us go and make our visit.

In the room the women come and go
Talking of Michelangelo.

The yellow fog that rubs its back upon the window-panes,
The yellow smoke that rubs its muzzle on the window-panes,
Licked its tongue into the corners of the evening,
Lingered upon the pools that stand in drains,
Let fall upon its back the soot that falls from chimneys,
Slipped by the terrace, made a sudden leap,
And seeing that it was a soft October night,
Curled once about the house, and fell asleep.

And indeed there will be time
For the yellow smoke that slides along the street
Rubbing its back upon the window-panes;
There will be time, there will be time
To prepare a face to meet the faces that you meet;
There will be time to murder and create,

And time for all the works and days of hands
That lift and drop a question on your plate;
Time for you and time for me,
And time yet for a hundred indecisions,
And for a hundred visions and revisions,
Before the taking of a toast and tea.

In the room the women come and go
Talking of Michelangelo.

And indeed there will be time
To wonder, 'Do I dare?' and, 'Do I dare?'
Time to turn back and descend the stair,
With a bald spot in the middle of my hair –
(They will say: 'How his hair is growing thin!')
My morning coat, my collar mounting firmly to the chin,
My necktie rich and modest, but asserted by a simple pin –
(They will say: 'But how his arms and legs are thin!')
Do I dare
Disturb the universe?
In a minute there is time
For decisions and revisions which a minute will reverse.

For I have known them all already, known them all –
Have known the evenings, mornings, afternoons,
I have measured out my life with coffee spoons;
I know the voices dying with a dying fall
Beneath the music from a farther room.
    So how should I presume?

And I have known the eyes already, known them all –
The eyes that fix you in a formulated phrase,
And when I am formulated, sprawling on a pin,
When I am pinned and wriggling on the wall,
Then how should I begin
To spit out all the butt-ends of my days and ways?
    And how should I presume?

And I have known the arms already, known them all –
Arms that are braceleted and white and bare
(But in the lamplight, downed with light brown hair!)
Is it perfume from a dress
That makes me so digress?
Arms that lie along a table, or wrap about a shawl.
    And should I then presume?
    And how should I begin?

      *   *   *

Shall I say, I have gone at dusk through narrow streets
And watched the smoke that rises from the pipes
Of lonely men in shirt-sleeves, leaning out of windows? . . .

I should have been a pair of ragged claws
Scuttling across the floors of silent seas.

      *   *   *

And the afternoon, the evening, sleeps so peacefully!
Smoothed by long fingers,
Asleep . . . tired . . . or it malingers,
Stretched on the floor, here beside you and me.
Should I, after tea and cakes and ices,
Have the strength to force the moment to its crisis?
But though I have wept and fasted, wept and prayed,
Though I have seen my head (grown slightly bald)
    brought in upon a platter,
I am no prophet – and here's no great matter;
I have seen the moment of my greatness flicker,
And I have seen the eternal Footman hold my coat, and snicker,
And in short, I was afraid.

And would it have been worth it, after all,
After the cups, the marmalade, the tea,
Among the porcelain, among some talk of you and me,
Would it have been worth while,
To have bitten off the matter with a smile,
To have squeezed the universe into a ball
To roll it towards some overwhelming question,
To say: 'I am Lazarus, come from the dead,
Come back to tell you all, I shall tell you all' –
If one, settling a pillow by her head,
    Should say: 'That is not what I meant at all.
    That is not it, at all.'

And would it have been worth it, after all,
Would it have been worth while,
After the sunsets and the dooryards and the sprinkled streets,
After the novels, after the teacups, after the skirts that trail along
   the floor –
And this, and so much more? –
It is impossible to say just what I mean!
But as if a magic lantern threw the nerves in patterns on a screen:
Would it have been worth while
If one, settling a pillow or throwing off a shawl,
And turning toward the window, should say:
   'That is not it at all,
   That is not what I meant, at all.'

     *   *   *

No! I am not Prince Hamlet, nor was meant to be;
Am an attendant lord, one that will do
To swell a progress, start a scene or two,
Advise the prince; no doubt, an easy tool,
Deferential, glad to be of use,
Politic, cautious, and meticulous;
Full of high sentence, but a bit obtuse;
At times, indeed, almost ridiculous –
Almost, at times, the Fool.

I grow old . . . I grow old . . .
I shall wear the bottoms of my trousers rolled.

Shall I part my hair behind? Do I dare to eat a peach?
I shall wear white flannel trousers, and walk upon the beach.
I have heard the mermaids singing, each to each.

I do not think that they will sing to me.

I have seen them riding seaward on the waves
Combing the white hair of the waves blown back
When the wind blows the water white and black.

We have lingered in the chambers of the sea
By sea-girls wreathed with seaweed red and brown
Till human voices wake us, and we drown.

—◦•◦—

T. S. ELIOT

Journey of the Magi

'A cold coming we had of it,
Just the worst time of the year
For a journey, and such a long journey:
The ways deep and the weather sharp,
The very dead of winter.'
And the camels galled, sore-footed, refractory,
Lying down in the melting snow.
There were times we regretted
The summer palaces on slopes, the terraces,
And the silken girls bringing sherbet.
Then the camel men cursing and grumbling
And running away, and wanting their liquor and women,
And the night-fires going out, and the lack of shelters,
And the cities hostile and the towns unfriendly
And the villages dirty and charging high prices:
A hard time we had of it.
At the end we preferred to travel all night,
Sleeping in snatches,
With the voices singing in our ears, saying
That this was all folly.

Then at dawn we came down to a temperate valley,
Wet, below the snow line, smelling of vegetation;
With a running stream and a water-mill beating the darkness,
And three trees on the low sky,
And an old white horse galloped away in the meadow.
Then we came to a tavern with vine-leaves over the lintel,
Six hands at an open door dicing for pieces of silver,
And feet kicking the empty wine-skins.
But there was no information, and so we continued
And arrived at evening, not a moment too soon
Finding the place; it was (you may say) satisfactory.

All this was a long time ago, I remember,
And I would do it again, but set down
This set down
This: were we led all that way for
Birth or Death? There was a Birth, certainly,
We had evidence and no doubt. I had seen birth and death,
But had thought they were different; this Birth was
Hard and bitter agony for us, like Death, our death.
We returned to our places, these Kingdoms,
But no longer at ease here, in the old dispensation,
With an alien people clutching their gods.
I should be glad of another death.

——◦◦——

T. S. Eliot

from *The Rubáiyát of Omar Khayyám*

Come, fill the Cup, and in the Fire of Spring
The Winter Garment of Repentance fling:
   The Bird of Time has but a little way
To fly – and Lo! the Bird is on the Wing.

And look – a thousand Blossoms with the Day
Woke – and a thousand scatter'd into Clay:
   And this first Summer Month that brings the Rose
Shall take Jamshýd and Kaikobád away.

But come with old Khayyám, and leave the Lot
Of Kaikobád and Kaikhosrú forgot:
   Let Rustum lay about him as he will,
Or Hátim Tai cry Supper – heed them not.

With me along some Strip of Herbage strown
That just divides the desert from the sown,
   Where name of slave and Sultán scarce is known,
And pity Sultán Máhmúd on his Throne.

Here with a Loaf of Bread beneath the Bough,
A Flask of Wine, a Book of Verse – and Thou
   Beside me singing in the Wilderness –
And Wilderness is Paradise enow.

          *   *   *

Myself when young did eagerly frequent
Doctor and Saint, and heard great Argument
   About it and about: but evermore
Came out by the same Door as in I went.

With them the Seed of Wisdom did I sow,
And with my own hand labour'd it to grow:
   And this was all the Harvest that I reap'd –
'I came like Water, and like Wind I go.'

          *   *   *

The Moving Finger writes; and, having writ,
Moves on: nor all thy Piety nor Wit
 Shall lure it back to cancel half a Line,
Nor all thy Tears wash out a Word of it.

And that inverted Bowl we call The Sky,
Whereunder crawling coop't we live and die,
 Lift not thy hands to *It* for help – for It
Rolls impotently on as Thou or I.

———◦◦———

EDWARD FITZGERALD

The Golden Journey to Samarkand

Prologue

We who with songs beguile your pilgrimage
And swear that Beauty lives though lilies die,
We Poets of the proud old lineage
Who sing to find your hearts, we know not why, –

What shall we tell you? Tales, marvellous tales
Of ships and stars and isles where good men rest,
Where nevermore the rose of sunset pales,
And winds and shadows fall toward the West:

And there the world's first huge white-bearded kings
In dim glades sleeping, murmur in their sleep,
And closer round their breasts the ivy clings,
Cutting its pathway slow and red and deep.

II

And how beguile you? Death has no repose
Warmer and deeper than that Orient sand
Which hides the beauty and bright faith of those
Who made the Golden Journey to Samarkand.

And now they wait and whiten peaceably,
Those conquerors, those poets, those so fair:
They know time comes, not only you and I,
But the whole world shall whiten, here or there;

When those long caravans that cross the plain
With dauntless feet and sound of silver bells
Put forth no more for glory or for gain,
Take no more solace from the palm-girt wells.

When the great markets by the sea shut fast
All that calm Sunday that goes on and on:
When even lovers find their peace at last,
And Earth is but a star, that once had shone.

JAMES ELROY FLECKER

Stopping by Woods on a Snowy Evening

Whose woods these are I think I know.
His house is in the village, though;
He will not see me stopping here
To watch his woods fill up with snow.

My little horse must think it queer
To stop without a farmhouse near
Between the woods and frozen lake
The darkest evening of the year.

He gives his harness bells a shake
To ask if there is some mistake.
The only other sound's the sweep
Of easy wind and downy flake.

The woods are lovely, dark, and deep,
But I have promises to keep,
And miles to go before I sleep,
And miles to go before I sleep.

ROBERT FROST

The Road Not Taken

Two roads diverged in a yellow wood,
And sorry I could not travel both
And be one traveler, long I stood
And looked down one as far as I could
To where it bent in the undergrowth;

Then took the other, as just as fair,
And having perhaps the better claim,
Because it was grassy and wanted wear;
Though as for that, the passing there
Had worn them really about the same,

And both that morning equally lay
In leaves no step had trodden black.
Oh, I kept the first for another day!
Yet knowing how way leads on to way,
I doubted if I should ever come back.

I shall be telling this with a sigh
Somewhere ages and ages hence:
Two roads diverged in a wood, and I –
I took the one less traveled by,
And that has made all the difference.

ROBERT FROST

Song

When lovely woman stoops to folly
And finds too late that men betray, –
What charm can soothe her melancholy,
What art can wash her guilt away?

The only art her guilt to cover,
To hide her shame from every eye
To give repentance to her lover
And wring his bosom, is – to die.

OLIVER GOLDSMITH

from *The Deserted Village*

Beside yon straggling fence that skirts the way,
With blossomed furze unprofitably gay,
There, in his noisy mansion, skilled to rule,
The village master taught his little school;
A man severe he was, and stern to view;
I knew him well, and every truant knew;
Well had the boding tremblers learned to trace
The day's disasters in his morning face;
Full well they laughed, with counterfeited glee,
At all his jokes, for many a joke had he;
Full well the busy whisper, circling round,
Conveyed the dismal tidings when he frowned;
Yet he was kind, or, if severe in aught,
The love he bore to learning was in fault;
The village all declared how much he knew;
'Twas certain he could write, and cipher too;
Lands he could measure, terms and tides presage,
And e'en the story ran that he could gauge.
In arguing too, the parson owned his skill,
For e'en though vanquished, he could argue still;
While words of learned length and thundering sound
Amazed the gazing rustics ranged around,
And still they gazed, and still the wonder grew,
That one small head could carry all he knew.

OLIVER GOLDSMITH

from *Ye Wearie Wayfarer*

Question not, but live and labour
　Till yon goal be won,
Helping every feeble neighbour,
　Seeking help from none;
Life is mostly froth and bubble,
　Two things stand like stone,
Kindness in another's trouble,
　Courage in your own.

ADAM LINDSAY GORDON

Elegy
Written in a Country Churchyard

The curfew tolls the knell of parting day,
The lowing herd wind slowly o'er the lea,
The ploughman homeward plods his weary way,
And leaves the world to darkness and to me.

Now fades the glimmering landscape on the sight,
And all the air a solemn stillness holds,
Save where the beetle wheels his droning flight,
And drowsy tinklings lull the distant folds:

Save that from yonder ivy-mantled tower
The moping owl does to the moon complain
Of such as, wandering near her secret bower,
Molest her ancient solitary reign.

Beneath those rugged elms, that yew-tree's shade
When heaves the turf in many a mouldering heap,
Each in his narrow cell for ever laid,
The rude Forefathers of the hamlet sleep.

The breezy call of incense-breathing morn,
The swallow twittering from the straw-built shed,
The cock's shrill clarion, or the echoing horn,
No more shall rouse them from their lowly bed.

For them no more the blazing hearth shall burn
Or busy housewife ply her evening care:
No children run to lisp their sire's return,
Or climb his knees the envied kiss to share.

Oft did the harvest to their sickle yield,
Their furrow oft the stubborn glebe has broke;
How jocund did they drive their team afield!
How bow'd the woods beneath their sturdy stroke!

Let not Ambition mock their useful toil,
Their homely joys, and destiny obscure;
Nor Grandeur hear with a disdainful smile
The short and simple annals of the Poor.

The boast of heraldry, the pomp of power,
And all that beauty, all that wealth e'er gave,
Awaits alike th' inevitable hour: –
The paths of glory lead but to the grave.

Nor you, ye Proud, impute to these the fault
If Memory o'er their tomb no trophies raise,
Where through the long-drawn aisle and fretted vault
The pealing anthem swells the note of praise.

Can storied urn or animated bust
Back to its mansion call the fleeting breath?
Can Honour's voice provoke the silent dust,
Or Flattery soothe the dull cold ear of Death?

Perhaps in this neglected spot is laid
Some heart once pregnant with celestial fire;
Hands, that the rod of empire might have sway'd,
Or waked to ecstasy the living lyre:

But Knowledge to their eyes her ample page
Rich with the spoils of time, did ne'er unroll;
Chill Penury repress'd their noble rage,
And froze the genial current of the soul.

Full many a gem of purest ray serene
The dark unfathom'd caves of ocean bear:
Full many a flower is born to blush unseen,
And waste its sweetness on the desert air.

Some village-Hampden, that with dauntless breast
The little tyrant of his fields withstood,
Some mute inglorious Milton here may rest,
Some Cromwell, guiltless of his country's blood.

Th' applause of list'ning senates to command,
The threats of pain and ruin to despise,
To scatter plenty o'er a smiling land,
And read their history in a nation's eyes

Their lot forbade: nor circumscribed alone
Their growing virtues, but their crimes confined;
Forbade to wade through slaughter to a throne,
And shut the gates of mercy on mankind;

The struggling pangs of conscious truth to hide,
To quench the blushes of ingenuous shame,
Or heap the shrine of Luxury and Pride
With incense kindled at the Muse's flame.

Far from the madding crowd's ignoble strife
Their sober wishes never learn'd to stray;
Along the cool sequester'd vale of life
They kept the noiseless tenor of their way.

Yet e'en these bones from insult to protect
Some frail memorial still erected nigh,
With uncouth rhymes and shapeless sculpture deck'd,
Implores the passing tribute of a sigh.

Their name, their years, spelt by th' unletter'd Muse,
The place of fame and elegy supply:
And many a holy text around she strews
That teach the rustic moralist to die.

For who, to dumb forgetfulness a prey,
This pleasing anxious being e'er resign'd,
Left the warm precincts of the cheerful day,
Nor cast one longing lingering look behind?

On some fond breast the parting soul relies,
Some pious drops the closing eye requires;
E'en from the tomb the voice of Nature cries,
E'en in our ashes live their wonted fires.

For thee, who, mindful of th' unhonour'd dead,
Dost in these lines their artless tale relate;
If chance, by lonely Contemplation led,
Some kindred spirit shall inquire thy fate, –

Haply some hoary-headed swain may say,
Oft have we seen him at the peep of dawn
Brushing with hasty steps the dews away,
To meet the sun upon the upland lawn;

There at the foot of yonder nodding beech
That wreathes its old fantastic roots so high,
His listless length at noon-tide would he stretch,
And pore upon the brook that babbles by.

Hard by yon wood, now smiling as in scorn,
Muttering his wayward fancies he would rove;
Now drooping, woeful-wan, like one forlorn,
Or crazed with care, or cross'd in hopeless love.

One morn I miss'd him on the custom'd hill,
Along the heath, and near his favourite tree;
Another came; nor yet beside the rill,
Nor up the lawn, nor at the wood was he;

The next with dirges due in sad array
Slow through the church-way path we saw him borne, ·
Approach and read (for thou canst read) the lay
Graved on the stone beneath yon aged thorn.

THE EPITAPH

Here rests his head upon the lap of Earth
A Youth, to Fortune and to Fame unknown;
Fair Science frown'd not on his humble birth,
And Melancholy mark'd him for her own.

Large was his bounty, and his soul sincere;
Heaven did a recompense as largely send:
He gave to Misery all he had, a tear,
He gain'd from Heaven, 'twas all he wish'd, a friend.

No farther seek his merits to disclose,
Or draw his frailties from their dread abode,
(There they alike in trembling hope repose)
The bosom of his Father and his God.

—•◇•—

THOMAS GRAY

The Green Eye of the Yellow God

There's a one-eyed yellow idol to the north of Khatmandu,
There's a little marble cross below the town;
There's a broken-hearted woman tends the grave of Mad Carew,
And the Yellow God forever gazes down.

He was known as Mad Carew by the subs of Khatmandu,
He was hotter than they felt inclined to tell;
But for all his foolish pranks, he was worshipped in the ranks,
And the Colonel's daughter smiled on him as well.

He had loved her all along, with a passion of the strong,
The fact that she loved him was plain to all.
She was nearly twenty-one and arrangements had begun
To celebrate her birthday with a ball.

He wrote to ask what present she would like from Mad Carew;
They met next day as he dismissed a squad;
And jestingly she told him then that nothing else would do
But the green eye of the little Yellow God.

On the night before the dance, Mad Carew seemed in a trance,
And they chaffed him as they puffed at their cigars;
But for once he failed to smile, and he sat alone awhile,
Then went out into the night beneath the stars.

He returned before the dawn, with his shirt and tunic torn,
And a gash across his temples dripping red;
He was patched up right away, and he slept through all the day,
And the Colonel's daughter watched beside his bed.

He woke at last and asked if they could send his tunic through;
She brought it, and he thanked her with a nod;
He bade her search the pocket, saying, 'That's from Mad Carew',
And she found the little green eye of the god.

She upbraided poor Carew in the way that women do,
Though both her eyes were strangely hot and wet;
But she wouldn't take the stone, and Mad Carew was left alone
With the jewel that he'd chanced his life to get.

When the ball was at its height, on that still and tropic night,
She thought of him and hastened to his room ;
As she crossed the barrack square she could hear the dreamy air
Of a waltz tune softly stealing through the gloom.

His door was open wide, with silver moonlight shining through,
The place was wet and slippery where she trod;
An ugly knife lay buried in the heart of Mad Carew,
'Twas the 'Vengeance of the Little Yellow God'.

There's a one-eyed yellow idol to the north of Khatmandu,
There's a little marble cross below the town;
There's a broken-hearted woman tends the grave of Mad Carew,
And the Yellow God forever gazes down.

—— ·o· ——

J. MILTON HAYES

Casabianca

The boy stood on the burning deck,
  Whence all but he had fled;
The flame that lit the battle's wreck
  Shone round him o'er the dead.

Yet beautiful and bright he stood,
  As born to rule the storm;
A creature of heroic blood,
  A brave though childlike form.

The flames roll'd on – he would not go
  Without his father's word;
That father, faint in death below,
  His voice no longer heard.

He call'd aloud – 'Say, father, say
  If yet my task is done!'
He knew not that the chieftain lay
  Unconscious of his son.

'Speak, father!' once again he cried,
  'If I may yet be gone;'
And but the booming shots replied,
  And fast the flames roll'd on.

Upon his brow he felt their breath,
  And in his waving hair,
And look'd from that lone post of death
  In still yet brave despair.

And shouted but once more aloud,
  'My father, must I stay?'
While o'er him fast, through sail and shroud,
  The wreathing fires made way.

They wrapp'd the ship in splendour wild,
    They caught the flag on high,
And stream'd above the gallant child,
    Like banners in the sky.

There came a burst of thunder-sound –
    The boy! – oh, where was he?
Ask of the winds, that far around
    With fragments strew'd the sea! –

With mast, and helm, and pennon fair,
    That well had borne their part;
But the noblest thing that perish'd there
    Was that young faithful heart.

———◆◆———

FELICIA HEMANS

Invictus

Out of the night that covers me,
  Black as the pit from pole to pole,
I thank whatever gods may be
  For my unconquerable soul.

In the fell clutch of circumstance
  I have not winced nor cried aloud.
Under the bludgeonings of chance
  My head is bloody, but unbowed.

Beyond this place of wrath and tears
  Looms but the Horror of the shade,
And yet the menace of the years
  Finds and shall find me unafraid.

It matters not how strait the gate,
  How charged with punishments the scroll,
I am the master of my fate:
  I am the captain of my soul.

WILLIAM ERNEST HENLEY

To the Virgins, to Make Much of Time

Gather ye rosebuds while ye may,
  Old Time is still a-flying:
And this same flower that smiles to-day
  To-morrow will be dying.

The glorious lamp of heaven, the sun,
  The higher he's a-getting,
The sooner will his race be run,
  And nearer he's to setting.

That age is best which is the first,
  When youth and blood are warmer;
But being spent, the worse, and worst
  Times still succeed the former.

Then be not coy, but use your time,
  And while ye may, go marry:
For having lost but once your prime,
  You may for ever tarry.

ROBERT HERRICK

To Daffodils

Fair daffodils, we weep to see
  You haste away so soon;
As yet the early-rising sun
  Has not attained his noon.
    Stay, stay
    Until the hasting day
    Has run
    But to the evensong;
And, having prayed together, we
  Will go with you along.

We have short time to stay as you,
  We have as short a spring;
As quick a growth to meet decay,
  As you, or anything.
    We die
    As your hours do, and dry
    Away
    Like to the summer's rain;
Or as the pearls of morning's dew,
  Ne'er to be found again.

ROBERT HERRICK

Time, You Old Gipsy Man

Time, you old gipsy man,
    Will you not stay,
Put up your caravan
    Just for one day?

All things I'll give you
Will you be my guest,
Bells for your jennet
Of silver the best,
Goldsmiths shall beat you
A great golden ring,
Peacocks shall bow to you,
Little boys sing,
Oh, and sweet girls will
Festoon you with may,
Time, you old gipsy,
Why hasten away?

Last week in Babylon,
Last night in Rome,
Morning, and in the crush
Under Paul's dome;
Under Paul's dial
You tighten your rein –
Only a moment,
And off once again;
Off to some city
Now blind in the womb,
Off to another
Ere that's in the tomb.

Time, you old gipsy man,
    Will you not stay,
Put up your caravan
    Just for one day?

RALPH HODGSON

I Remember, I Remember

I remember, I remember,
The house where I was born,
The little window where the sun
Came peeping in at morn;
He never came a wink too soon,
Nor brought too long a day,
But now, I often wish the night
Had borne my breath away!

I remember, I remember,
The roses, red and white,
The violets, and the lily-cups,
Those flowers made of light!
The lilacs where the robin built,
And where my brother set
The laburnum on his birthday, –
The tree is living yet!

I remember, I remember,
Where I was used to swing,
And thought the air must rush as fresh
To swallows on the wing;
My spirit flew in feathers then,
That is so heavy now,
And summer pools could hardly cool
The fever on my brow!

I remember, I remember,
The fir trees dark and high;
I used to think their slender tops
Were close against the sky:
It was a childish ignorance,
But now 'tis little joy
To know I'm farther off from heaven
Than when I was a boy.

THOMAS HOOD

The Song of the Shirt

With fingers weary and worn,
   With eyelids heavy and red,
A woman sat, in unwomanly rags,
   Plying her needle and thread –
Stitch! stitch! stitch!
   In poverty, hunger, and dirt,
And still with a voice of dolorous pitch
   She sang the 'Song of the Shirt.'

'Work! work! work!
   While the cock is crowing aloof!
And work – work – work,
   Till the stars shine through the roof!
It's Oh! to be a slave
   Along with the barbarous Turk,
Where woman has never a soul to save,
   If this is Christian work.

'Work – work – work,
   Till the brain begins to swim;
Work – work – work,
   Till the eyes are heavy and dim!
Seam, and gusset, and band,
   Band, and gusset, and seam,
Till over the buttons I fall asleep,
   And sew them on in a dream!

'Oh, Men, with Sisters dear!
   Oh, Men, with Mothers and Wives!
It is not linen you're wearing out
   But human creatures' lives!
Stitch – stitch – stitch,
   In poverty, hunger, and dirt,
Sewing at once, with a double thread,
   A Shroud as well as a Shirt.

'But why do I talk of Death?
    That Phantom of grisly bone,
I hardly fear its terrible shape,
    It seems so like my own –
It seems so like my own,
    Because of the fasts I keep;
Oh, God, that bread should be so dear,
    And flesh and blood so cheap!

'Work – work – work!
    My labour never flags;
And what are its wages? A bed of straw,
    A crust of bread – and rags.
That shattered roof – this naked floor –
    A table – a broken chair –
And a wall so blank, my shadow I thank
    For sometimes falling there!

'Work – work – work!
    From weary chime to chime,
Work – work – work,
    As prisoners work for crime!
Band, and gusset, and seam,
    Seam, and gusset, and band,
Till the heart is sick, and the brain benumbed,
    As well as the weary hand.

'Work – work – work!
    In the dull December light,
And work – work – work,
    When the weather is warm and bright –
While underneath the eaves
    The brooding swallows cling
As if to show me their sunny backs
    And twit me with the spring.

'Oh! but to breathe the breath
    Of the cowslip and primrose sweet –
With the sky above my head,
    And the grass beneath my feet;
For only one short hour
    To feel as I used to feel,
Before I knew the woes of want
    And the walk that costs a meal.

'Oh! but for one short hour!
    A respite however brief!
No blessèd leisure for Love or Hope,
    But only time for Grief!
A little weeping would ease my heart,
    But in their briny bed
My tears must stop, for every drop
    Hinders needle and thread!'

With fingers weary and worn,
    With eyelids heavy and red,
A woman sat, in unwomanly rags,
    Plying her needle and thread –
Stitch! stitch! stitch!
    In poverty, hunger, and dirt,
And still with a voice of dolorous pitch, –
Would that its tone could reach the Rich! –
    She sang this 'Song of the Shirt!'

——◦◦——

THOMAS HOOD

Pied Beauty

Glory be to God for dappled things –
  For skies of couple-colour as a brinded cow;
    For rose-moles all in stipple upon trout that swim;
Fresh-firecoal chestnut-falls; finches' wings;
  Landscape plotted and pierced – fold, fallow, and plough;
  And all trades, their gear and tackle and trim.

All things counter, original, spare, strange;
  Whatever is fickle, freckled (who knows how?)
    With swift, slow; sweet, sour; adazzle, dim;
He fathers-forth whose beauty is past change:
      Praise him.

GERALD MANLEY HOPKINS

Loveliest of Trees, the Cherry now

Loveliest of trees, the cherry now
Is hung with bloom along the bough,
And stands about the woodland ride
Wearing white for Eastertide.

Now, of my threescore years and ten,
Twenty will not come again,
And take from seventy springs a score,
It only leaves me fifty more.

And since to look at things in bloom
Fifty springs are little room,
About the woodlands I will go
To see the cherry hung with snow.

A. E. HOUSMAN

In Summertime on Bredon

In summertime on Bredon
  The bells they sound so clear;
Round both the shires they ring them
  In steeples far and near,
  A happy noise to hear.

Here of a Sunday morning
  My love and I would lie,
And see the coloured counties,
  And hear the larks so high
  About us in the sky.

The bells would ring to call her
  In valleys miles away:
'Come all to church, good people;
  Good people, come and pray.'
  But here my love would stay.

And I would turn and answer
  Among the springing thyme,
'Oh, peal upon our wedding,
  And we will hear the chime,
  And come to church in time.'

But when the snows at Christmas
  On Bredon top were strown,
My love rose up so early
  And stole out unbeknown
  And went to church alone.

They tolled the one bell only,
  Groom there was none to see,
The mourners followed after,
  And so to church went she,
  And would not wait for me.

The bells they sound on Bredon,
   And still the steeples hum.
'Come all to church, good people,' –
   Oh, noisy bells, be dumb;
   I hear you, I will come.

———◦—

A. E. HOUSMAN

Battle Hymn of the American Republic

Mine eyes have seen the glory of the coming of the Lord;
He is trampling out the vintage where the grapes of wrath are
  stored;
He hath loosed the fatal lightning of his terrible swift sword:
  His Truth is marching on.

I have seen him in the watch-fires of a hundred circling camps;
They have builded him an altar in the evening dews and damps;
I have read his righteous sentence by the dim and flaring lamps:
  His Day is marching on.

I have read a fiery gospel, writ in burnished rows of steel:
'As you deal with my contemners, so with you my grace shall
  deal;'
Let the Hero born of woman crush the serpent with his heel,
  Since God is marching on.

He has sounded forth the trumpet that shall never call retreat;
He is sifting out the hearts of men before his judgment-seat;
O be swift, my soul, to answer him; be jubilant, my feet!
  Our God is marching on.

In the beauty of the lilies Christ was born across the sea,
With a glory in his bosom that transfigures you and me;
As he died to make men holy, let us die to make men free,
  While God is marching on.

He is coming like the glory of the morning on the wave;
He is wisdom to the mighty, he is succour to the brave;
So the world shall be his footstool, and the soul of time his slave;
  Our God is marching on.

JULIA WARD HOWE

Abou Ben Adhem and the Angel

Abou Ben Adhem (may his tribe increase!)
Awoke one night from a deep dream of peace,
And saw, within the moonlight in his room,
Making it rich, and like a lily in bloom,
An angel writing in a book of gold: –
Exceeding peace had made Ben Adhem bold,
And to the presence in the room he said,
 'What writest thou?' – The vision raised its head,
And with a look made of all sweet accord,
Answered, 'The names of those who love the Lord.'
'And is mine one?' said Abou. 'Nay, not so,'
Replied the angel. Abou spoke more low,
But cheerly still; and said, 'I pray thee, then,
Write me as one that loves his fellow men.'
 The angel wrote, and vanished. The next night
It came again with a great wakening light,
And showed the names whom love of God had blest,
And lo! Ben Adhem's name led all the rest.

Leigh Hunt

To Celia

Drink to me only with thine eyes,
   And I will pledge with mine;
Or leave a kiss but in the cup
   And I'll not look for wine.
The thirst that from the soul doth rise
   Doth ask a drink divine;
But might I of Jove's nectar sup,
   I would not change for thine.

I sent thee late a rosy wreath,
   Not so much honouring thee
As giving it a hope that there
   It could not wither'd be;
But thou thereon didst only breathe
   And sent'st it back to me;
Since when it grows, and smells, I swear,
   Not of itself but thee!

BEN JONSON

Hymn to Diana

Queen and Huntress, chaste and fair,
  Now the sun is laid to sleep,
Seated in thy silver chair
  State in wonted manner keep:
    Hesperus entreats thy light,
    Goddess excellently bright.

Earth, let not thy envious shade
  Dare itself to interpose;
Cynthia's shining orb was made
  Heaven to clear when day did close:
    Bless us then with wishèd sight,
    Goddess excellently bright.

Lay thy bow of pearl apart
  And the crystal-shining quiver;
Give unto the flying hart
  Space to breathe, how short soever:
    Thou that mak'st a day of night,
    Goddess excellently bright!

BEN JONSON

On First Looking into Chapman's Homer

Much have I travelled in the realms of gold,
  And many goodly states and kingdoms seen;
  Round many western islands have I been
Which bards in fealty to Apollo hold.
Oft of one wide expanse had I been told
  That deep-browed Homer ruled as his demesne:
  Yet did I never breathe its pure serene
Till I heard Chapman speak out loud and bold:
Then felt I like some watcher of the skies
  When a new planet swims into his ken;
Or like stout Cortez, when with eagle eyes
  He stared at the Pacific – and all his men
Looked at each other with a wild surmise –
  Silent, upon a peak in Darien.

JOHN KEATS

To Autumn

Season of mists and mellow fruitfulness,
Close bosom-friend of the maturing sun;
Conspiring with him how to load and bless
With fruit the vines that round the thatch-eaves run;
To bend with apples the moss'd cottage-trees,
And fill all fruit with ripeness to the core;
To swell the gourd, and plump the hazel shells
With a sweet kernel; to set budding more,
And still more, later flowers for the bees,
Until they think warm days will never cease,
For Summer has o'er-brimm'd their clammy cells.

Who hath not seen thee oft amid thy store?
Sometimes whoever seeks abroad may find
Thee sitting careless on a granary floor,
Thy hair soft-lifted by the winnowing wind;
Or on a half-reap'd furrow sound asleep,
Drows'd with the fume of poppies, while thy hook
Spares the next swath and all its twinèd flowers:
And sometimes like a gleaner thou dost keep
Steady thy laden head across a brook;
Or by a cyder-press, with patient look,
Thou watchest the last oozings hours by hours.

Where are the songs of Spring? Ay, where are they?
Think not of them, thou hast thy music too, –
While barred clouds bloom the soft-dying day,
And touch the stubble-plains with rosy hue;
Then in a wailful choir the small gnats mourn
Among the river sallows, borne aloft
Or sinking as the light wind lives or dies;
And full-grown lambs loud bleat from hilly bourne;
Hedge-crickets sing; and now with treble soft
The red-breast whistles from a garden-croft;
And gathering swallows twitter in the skies.

JOHN KEATS

La Belle Dame Sans Merci

O what can ail thee, knight-at-arms,
Alone and palely loitering?
The sedge is wither'd from the lake,
And no birds sing.

'O what can ail thee, knight-at-arms,
So haggard and so woe-begone?
The squirrel's granary is full,
And the harvest's done.

'I see a lily on thy brow
With anguish moist and fever dew;
And on thy cheek a fading rose
Fast withereth too.'

'I met a lady in the meads,
Full beautiful – a faery's child,
Her hair was long, her foot was light,
And her eyes were wild.

'I made a garland for her head,
And bracelets too, and fragrant zone;
She look'd at me as she did love,
And made sweet moan.

'I set her on my pacing steed
And nothing else saw all day long,
For sideways would she lean and sing
A faery's song.

'She found me roots of relish sweet,
And honey wild and manna dew,
And sure in language strange she said,
"I love thee true!"

'She took me to her elfin grot,
And there she wept and sigh'd full sore;
And there I shut her wild, wild eyes
With kisses four.

'And there she lullèd me asleep,
And there I dream'd – Ah! woe betide!
The latest dream I ever dream'd
On the cold hill's side.

'I saw pale kings and princes too,
Pale warriors, death-pale were they all;
Who cried – "La belle Dame sans Merci
Hath thee in thrall!"

'I saw their starved lips in the gloam
With horrid warning gapèd wide,
And I awoke and found me here
On the cold hill's side.

'And this is why I sojourn here
Alone and palely loitering,
Though the sedge is wither'd from the lake,
And no birds sing.'

———◦◦———

JOHN KEATS

Ode to a Nightingale

My heart aches, and a drowsy numbness pains
 My sense, as though of hemlock I had drunk,
Or emptied some dull opiate to the drains
 One minute past, and Lethe-wards had sunk:
'Tis not through envy of thy happy lot,
 But being too happy in thy happiness, –
 That thou, light-wingèd Dryad of the trees,
 In some melodious plot
Of beechen green, and shadows numberless,
 Singest of summer in full-throated ease.

O for a draught of vintage! that hath been
 Cool'd a long age in the deep-delvèd earth,
Tasting of Flora and the country-green,
 Dance, and Provençal song, and sunburnt mirth.
O for a beaker full of the warm South,
 Full of the true, the blushful Hippocrene,
 With beaded bubbles winking at the brim
 And purple-stainèd mouth;
That I might drink, and leave the world unseen,
 And with thee fade away into the forest dim.

Fade far away, dissolve, and quite forget
 What thou among the leaves hast never known,
The weariness, the fever, and the fret
 Here, where men sit and hear each other groan;
Where palsy shakes a few, sad, last grey hairs,
 Where youth grows pale, and spectre-thin, and dies;
 Where but to think is to be full of sorrow
 And leaden-eyed despairs;
Where Beauty cannot keep her lustrous eyes,
 Or new Love pine at them beyond tomorrow.

Away! away! for I will fly to thee,
   Not charioted by Bacchus and his pards,
But on the viewless wings of Poesy,
   Though the dull brain perplexes and retards:
Already with thee! tender is the night,
   And haply the Queen-Moon is on her throne,
      Cluster'd around by all her starry Fays;
         But here there is no light
   Save what from heaven is with the breezes blown
      Through verdurous glooms and winding mossy ways.

I cannot see what flowers are at my feet,
   Nor what soft incense hangs upon the boughs,
But, in embalmèd darkness, guess each sweet
   Wherewith the seasonable month endows
The grass, the thicket, and the fruit-tree wild;
   White hawthorn, and the pastoral eglantine;
      Fast-fading violets cover'd up in leaves;
         And mid-May's eldest child
   The coming musk-rose, full of dewy wine,
      The murmurous haunt of flies on summer eves.

Darkling I listen; and for many a time
   I have been half in love with easeful Death,
Call'd him soft names in many a musèd rhyme,
   To take into the air my quiet breath;
Now more than ever seems it rich to die,
   To cease upon the midnight with no pain,
      While thou art pouring forth thy soul abroad
         In such an ecstasy!
   Still wouldst thou sing, and I have ears in vain –
      To thy high requiem become a sod.

Thou wast not born for death, immortal Bird!
   No hungry generations tread thee down;
The voice I hear this passing night was heard
   In ancient days by emperor and clown:
Perhaps the selfsame song that found a path
   Through the sad heart of Ruth, when, sick for home,
      She stood in tears amid the alien corn;
         The same that oft-times hath
   Charm'd magic casements, opening on the foam
      Of perilous seas, in faery lands forlorn.

Forlorn! the very word is like a bell
    To toll me back from thee to my sole self!
Adieu! the fancy cannot cheat so well
    As she is famed to do, deceiving elf.
Adieu! adieu! thy plaintive anthem fades
    Past the near meadows, over the still stream,
        Up the hill-side; and now 'tis buried deep
                In the next valley-glades:
    Was it a vision, or a waking dream?
        Fled is that music: – do I wake or sleep?

————◦◦•————

JOHN KEATS

Trees

I think that I shall never see
A poem lovely as a tree.

A tree whose hungry mouth is prest
Against the earth's sweet flowing breast;

A tree that looks at God all day,
And lifts her leafy arms to pray;

A tree that may in Summer wear
A nest of robins in her hair;

Upon whose bosom snow has lain;
Who intimately lives with rain.

Poems are made by fools like me,
But only God can make a tree.

JOYCE KILMER

Young and Old

When all the world is young, lad,
  And all the trees are green;
And every goose a swan, lad,
  And every lass a queen;
Then hey for boot and horse, lad,
  And round the world away;
Young blood must have its course, lad,
  And every dog his day.

When all the world is old, lad,
  And all the trees are brown;
And all the sport is stale, lad,
  And all the wheels run down;
Creep home, and take your place there,
  The spent and maimed among:
God grant you find one face there,
  You loved when all was young.

CHARLES KINGSLEY

The Sands of Dee

'O Mary, go and call the cattle home,
    And call the cattle home,
    And call the cattle home
  Across the sands of Dee;'
The western wind was wild and dank with foam,
  And all alone went she.

The western tide crept up along the sand,
    And o'er and o'er the sand,
    And round and round the sand,
  As far as eye could see.
The rolling mist came down and hid the land:
  And never home came she.

'Oh! is it weed, or fish, or floating hair –
    A tress of golden hair,
    A drownèd maiden's hair
  Above the nets at sea?
Was never salmon yet that shone so fair
  Among the stakes on Dee.'

They rowed her in across the rolling foam,
    The cruel crawling foam,
    The cruel hungry foam,
  To her grave beside the sea:
But still the boatman hear her call the cattle home
  Across the sands of Dee.

CHARLES KINGSLEY

The Three Fishers

Three fishers went sailing away to the West,
   Away to the West as the sun went down;
Each thought on the woman who loved him the best,
   And the children stood watching them out of the town;
   For men must work, and women must weep,
   And there's little to earn, and many to keep,
      Though the harbour bar be moaning.

Three wives sat up in the lighthouse tower,
   And they trimmed the lamps as the sun went down;
They looked at the squall, and they looked at the shower,
   And the night-rack came rolling up ragged and brown.
   But men must work, and women must weep,
   Though storms be sudden, and waters deep,
      And the harbour bar be moaning.

Three corpses lay out on the shining sands
   In the morning gleam as the tide went down,
And the women are weeping and wringing their hands
   For those who will never come home to the town;
   For men must work, and women must weep,
   And the sooner it's over, the sooner to sleep;
      And good-bye to the bar and its moaning.

CHARLES KINGSLEY

If

—•••—

If you can keep your head when all about you
   Are losing theirs and blaming it on you,
If you can trust yourself when all men doubt you,
   But make allowance for their doubting too;
If you can wait and not be tired by waiting,
   Or being lied about, don't deal in lies,
Or being hated, don't give way to hating,
   And yet don't look too good, nor talk too wise:

If you can dream – and not make dreams your master;
   If you can think – and not make thoughts your aim;
If you can meet with Triumph and Disaster
   And treat those two imposters just the same;
If you can bear to hear the truth you've spoken
   Twisted by knaves to make a trap for fools,
Or watch the things you gave your life to, broken,
   And stoop and build 'em up with worn-out tools:

If you can make one heap of all your winnings
   And risk it on one turn of pitch-and-toss,
And lose, and start again at your beginnings
   And never breathe a word about your loss;
If you can force your heart and nerve and sinew
   To serve your turn long after they are gone,
And so hold on when there is nothing in you
   Except the Will which says to them: 'Hold on!'

If you can talk with crowds and keep your virtue,
   Or walk with Kings nor lose the common touch,
If neither foes nor loving friends can hurt you,
   If all men count with you, but none too much;
If you can fill the unforgiving minute
   With sixty seconds' worth of distance run,
Yours is the Earth and everything that's in it,
   And – which is more – you'll be a Man, my son!

—•◦•—

RUDYARD KIPLING

Boots

We're foot – slog – slog – slog – sloggin' over Africa –
Foot – foot – foot – foot – sloggin' over Africa –
(Boots – boots – boots – boots – movin' up and down again!)
    There's no discharge in the war!

Seven – six – eleven – five – nine-an'-twenty mile to-day –
Four – eleven – seventeen – thirty-two the day before –
(Boots – boots – boots – boots – movin' up and down again!)
    There's no discharge in the war!

Don't – don't – don't – don't – look at what's in front of you.
(Boots – boots – boots – boots – movin' up an' down again);
Men – men – men – men – men go mad with watchin' 'em,
    An' there's no discharge in the war!

Try – try – try – try – to think o' something different –
Oh – my – God – keep – me from goin' lunatic!
(Boots – boots – boots – boots – movin' up an' down again)
    There's no discharge in the war!

Count – count – count – count – the bullets in the bandoliers.
If – your – eyes – drop – they will get atop o' you!
(Boots – boots – boots – boots – movin' up and down again) –
    There's no discharge in the war!

We – can – stick – out – 'unger, thirst, an' weariness,
But – not – not – not – not the chronic sight of 'em –
Boots – boots – boots – boots – movin' up an' down again,
    An' there's no discharge in the war!

'T'ain't – so – bad – by – day because o' company,
But night – brings – long – strings – o' forty thousand million
Boots – boots – boots – boots – movin' up an' down again.
    There's no discharge in the war!

I – 'ave – marched – six – weeks in 'Ell an' certify
It – is – not – fire – devils, dark or anything,
But boots – boots – boots – boots – movin' up an' down again,
    An' there's no discharge in the war!

RUDYARD KIPLING

The Old Familiar Faces

I have had playmates, I have had companions,
In my days of childhood, in my joyful school-days,
All, all are gone, the old familiar faces.

I have been laughing, I have been carousing,
Drinking late, sitting late, with my bosom cronies,
All, all are gone, the old familiar faces.

I loved a love once, fairest among women:
Closed are her doors on me, I must not see her –
All, all are gone, the old familiar faces.

I have a friend, a kinder friend has no man;
Like an ingrate, I left my friend abruptly;
Left him, to muse on the old familiar faces.

Ghost-like I paced round the haunts of my childhood,
Earth seemed a desert I was bound to traverse,
Seeking to find the old familiar faces.

Friend of my bosom, thou more than a brother,
Why wert not thou born in my father's dwelling?
So might we talk of the old familiar faces –

How some they had died, and some they have left me,
And some are taken from me; all are departed;
All, all are gone, the old familiar faces.

CHARLES LAMB

Finis

———◆●◆———

I strove with none, for none was worth my strife:
Nature I loved, and next to Nature, Art:
I warm'd both hands before the fire of Life;
It sinks; and I am ready to depart.

———◆◦◆———

WALTER SAVAGE LANDOR

The Whitsun Weddings

That Whitsun, I was late getting away:
  Not till about
One-twenty on the sunlit Saturday
Did my three-quarters-empty train pull out,
All windows down, all cushions hot, all sense
Of being in a hurry gone. We ran
Behind the backs of houses, crossed a street
Of blinding windscreens, smelt the fish-dock; thence
The river's level drifting breadth began,
Where sky and Lincolnshire and water meet.

All afternoon, through the tall heat that slept
  For miles inland,
A slow and stopping curve southwards we kept.
Wide farms went by, short-shadowed cattle, and
Canals with floatings of industrial froth;
A hothouse flashed uniquely: hedges dipped
And rose: and now and then a smell of grass
Displaced the reek of buttoned carriage-cloth
Until the next town, new and nondescript,
Approached with acres of dismantled cars.

At first, I didn't notice what a noise
  The weddings made
Each station that we stopped at: sun destroys
The interest of what's happening in the shade,
And down the long cool platforms whoops and skirls
I took for porters larking with the mails,
And went on reading. Once we started, though,
We passed them, grinning and pomaded, girls
In parodies of fashion, heels and veils,
All posed irresolutely, watching us go,

As if out on the end of an event
   Waving goodbye
To something that survived it. Struck, I leant
More promptly out next time, more curiously,
And saw it all again in different terms:
The fathers with broad belts under their suits
And seamy foreheads; mothers loud and fat;
An uncle shouting smut; and then the perms,
The nylon gloves and jewellery-substitutes,
The lemons, mauves, and olive-ochres that

Marked off the girls unreally from the rest.
   Yes, from cafés
And banquet-halls up yards, and bunting-dressed
Coach-party annexes, the wedding-days
Were coming to an end. All down the line
Fresh couples climbed aboard: the rest stood round;
The last confetti and advice were thrown,
And, as we moved, each face seemed to define
Just what it saw departing: children frowned
At something dull; fathers had never known

Success so huge and wholly farcical;
   The women shared
The secret like a happy funeral;
While girls, gripping their handbags tighter, stared
At a religious wounding. Free at last,
And loaded with the sum of all they saw,
We hurried towards London, shuffling gouts of steam.
Now fields were building-plots, and poplars cast
Long shadows over major roads, and for
Some fifty minutes, that in time would seem

Just long enough to settle hats and say
   I nearly died,
A dozen marriages got under way.
They watched the landscape, sitting side by side
– An Odeon went past, a cooling tower,
And someone running up to bowl – and none
Thought of the others they would never meet
Or how their lives would all contain this hour.
I thought of London spread out in the sun,
Its postal districts packed like squares of wheat:

There we were aimed. And as we raced across
   Bright knots of rail
Past standing Pullmans, walls of blackened moss
Came close, and it was nearly done, this frail
Travelling coincidence; and what it held
Stood ready to be loosed with all the power
That being changed can give. We slowed again,
And as the tightened brakes took hold, there swelled
A sense of falling, like an arrow-shower
Sent out of sight, somewhere becoming rain.

—◆—

PHILIP LARKIN

The Owl and the Pussy-Cat

The Owl and the Pussy-Cat went to sea
   In a beautiful pea-green boat.
They took some honey, and plenty of money
   Wrapped up in a five-pound note.
The Owl looked up to the stars above,
   And sang to a small guitar,
'O lovely Pussy! O Pussy, my love,
What a beautiful Pussy you are,
      You are,
      You are!
What a beautiful Pussy you are!'

Pussy said to the Owl, 'You elegant fowl!
   How charmingly sweet you sing!
O let us be married! too long we have tarried:
   But what shall we do for a ring?'
They sailed away, for a year and a day,
   To the land where the Bong-Tree grows,
And there in a wood a Piggy-wig stood,
With a ring at the end of his nose,
      His nose,
      His nose!
With a ring at the end of his nose.

'Dear Pig, are you willing to sell for one shilling
   Your ring?' Said the Piggy, 'I will.'
So they took it away, and were married next day
   By the Turkey who lives on the hill.
They dined on mince, and slices of quince,
   Which they ate with a runcible spoon;
And hand in hand, on the edge of the sand
   They danced by the light of the moon,
      The moon,
      The moon,
They danced by the light of the moon.

EDWARD LEAR

The Arrow and the Song

I shot an arrow into the air,
It fell to earth, I knew not where;
For, so swiftly it flew, the sight
Could not follow it in its flight.

I breathed a song into the air,
It fell to earth, I knew not where;
For who has sight so keen and strong,
That it can follow the flight of song?

Long, long afterward, in an oak
I found the arrow, still unbroke;
And the song, from beginning to end,
I found again in the heart of a friend.

HENRY WADSWORTH LONGFELLOW

The Village Blacksmith

Under a spreading chestnut tree
  The village smithy stands;
The smith, a mighty man is he,
  With large and sinewy hands;
And the muscles of his brawny arms
  Are strong as iron bands.

His hair is crisp, and black, and long,
  His face is like the tan;
His brow is wet with honest sweat,
  He earns whate'er he can,
And looks the whole world in the face,
  For he owes not any man.

Week in, week out, from morn till night,
  You can hear his bellows blow;
You can hear him swing his heavy sledge,
  With measured beat and slow,
Like a sexton ringing the village bell,
  When the evening sun is low.

And children coming home from school
  Look in at the open door;
They love to see the flaming forge,
  And hear the bellows roar,
And catch the burning sparks that fly
Like chaff from a threshing floor.

He goes on Sunday to the church,
  And sits among his boys;
He hears the parson pray and preach,
  He hears his daughter's voice,
Singing in the village choir,
  And it makes his heart rejoice.

It sounds to him like her mother's voice,
    Singing in Paradise!
He needs must think of her once more,
    How in the grave she lies;
And with his hard, rough hand he wipes
    A tear out of his eyes.

Toiling, – rejoicing, – sorrowing,
    Onward through life he goes;
Each morning sees some task begin,
    Each evening sees it close;
Something attempted, something done,
    Has earned a night's repose.

Thanks, thanks to thee, my worthy friend,
    For the lesson thou hast taught!
Thus at the flaming forge of life
    Our fortunes must be wrought;
Thus on its sounding anvil shaped
    Each burning deed and thought!

———◦———

HENRY WADSWORTH LONGFELLOW

The Wreck of the Hesperus

It was the schooner Hesperus,
   That sailed the wintry sea;
And the skipper had taken his little daughter,
   To bear him company.

Blue were her eyes as the fairy-flax,
   Her cheeks like the dawn of day,
And her bosom white as the hawthorn buds
   That ope in the month of May.

The skipper he stood beside the helm,
   His pipe was in his mouth,
And he watched how the veering flaw did blow
   The smoke now West, now South.

Then up and spake an old Sailor,
   Had sailed the Spanish Main,
'I pray thee, put into yonder port,
   For I fear a hurricane.

'Last night the moon had a golden ring,
   And to-night no moon we see!'
The skipper he blew a whiff from his pipe,
   And a scornful laugh laughed he.

Colder and colder blew the wind,
   A gale from the North-east;
The snow fell hissing in the brine,
   And the billows frothed like yeast.

Down came the storm, and smote amain,
   The vessel in its strength;
She shuddered and paused, like a frightened steed,
   Then leaped her cable's length.

'Come hither! come hither! my little daughter,
   And do not tremble so ;
For I can weather the roughest gale,
   That ever wind did blow.'

He wrapped her warm in his seaman's coat
   Against the stinging blast;
He cut a rope from a broken spar,
   And bound her to the mast.

'O father! I hear the churchbells ring,
   O say, what may it be?'
''Tis a fog-bell on a rock-bound coast!' –
   And he steered for the open sea.

'O father! I hear the sound of guns,
   O say, what may it be?'
'Some ship in distress, that cannot live
   In such an angry sea!'

'O father! I see a gleaming light,
   O say, what may it be?'
But the father answered never a word,
   A frozen corpse was he.

Lashed to the helm, all stiff and stark,
   With his face turned to the skies,
The lantern gleamed through the gleaming snow
   On his fixed and glassy eyes.

Then the maiden clasped her hands and prayed
   That savèd she might be;
And she thought of Christ, who stilled the wave,
   On the Lake of Galilee.

And fast through the midnight dark and drear,
   Through the whistling sleet and snow,
Like a sheeted ghost, the vessel swept
   Towards the reef of Norman's Woe.

And ever the fitful gusts between
   A sound came from the land;
It was the sound of the trampling surf,
   On the rocks and the hard sea-sand.

The breakers were right beneath her bows,
   She drifted a dreary wreck,
And a whooping billow swept the crew
   Like icicles from her deck.

She struck where the white and fleecy waves
  Looked soft as carded wool,
But the cruel rocks, they gored her side
  Like the horns of an angry bull.

Her rattling shrouds, all sheathed in ice,
  With the masts went by the board;
Like a vessel of glass, she stove and sank,
  Ho! ho! the breakers roared!

At daybreak, on the bleak sea-beach,
  A fisherman stood aghast,
To see the form of a maiden fair,
  Lashed close to a drifting mast.

The salt sea was frozen on her breast,
  The salt tears in her eyes;
And he saw her hair, like the brown sea-weed,
  On the billows fall and rise.

Such was the wreck of the Hesperus,
  In the midnight and the snow!
Christ save us all from a death like this
  On the reef of Norman's Woe!

———◆———

HENRY WADSWORTH LONGFELLOW

To Lucasta, Going to the Wars

Tell me not, sweet, I am unkind,
　　That from the nunnery
Of thy chaste breast and quiet mind,
　　To war and arms I fly.

True, a new mistress now I chase,
　　The first foe in the field;
And with a stronger faith embrace
　　A sword, a horse, a shield.

Yet this inconstancy is such
　　As you too shall adore;
I could not love thee, dear, so much,
　　Lov'd I not Honour more.

RICHARD LOVELACE

To Althea, from Prison

When Love with unconfinèd wings
   Hovers within my gates,
And my divine Althea brings
   To whisper at the grates;
When I lie tangled in her hair
   And fetter'd to her eye,
The birds that wanton in the air
   Know no such liberty.

When flowing cups run swiftly round
   With no allaying Thames,
Our careless heads with roses crown'd,
   Our hearts with loyal flames;
When thirsty grief in wine we steep,
   When healths and draughts go free –
Fishes that tipple in the deep
   Know no such liberty.

When, linnet-like confinèd, I
   With shriller throat shall sing
The sweetness, mercy, majesty
   And glories of my King;
When I shall voice aloud how good
   He is, how great should be,
Enlargèd winds, that curl the flood,
   Know no such liberty.

Stone walls do not a prison make,
   Nor iron bars a cage;
Minds innocent and quiet take
   That for an hermitage:
If I have freedom in my love
   And in my soul am free,
Angels alone, that soar above,
   Enjoy such liberty.

RICHARD LOVELACE

Bagpipe Music

It's no go the merrygoround, it's no go the rickshaw,
All we want is a limousine and a ticket for the peepshow.
Their knickers are made of crêpe-de-chine, their shoes are made
of python,
Their halls are lined with tiger rugs and their walls with heads of
bison.

John MacDonald found a corpse, put it under the sofa,
Waited till it came to life and hit it with a poker,
Sold its eyes for souvenirs, sold its blood for whisky,
Kept its bones for dumb-bells to use when he was fifty.

It's no go the Yogi-Man, it's no go Blavatsky,
All we want is a bank balance and a bit of skirt in a taxi.

Annie MacDougall went to milk, caught her foot in the heather,
Woke to hear a dance record playing of Old Vienna.
It's no go your maidenheads, it's no go your culture,
All we want is a Dunlop tyre and the devil mend the puncture.

The Laird o'Phelps spent Hogmanay declaring he was sober,
Counted his feet to prove the fact and found he had one foot over.
Mrs Carmichael had her fifth, looked at the job with repulsion,
Said to the midwife 'Take it away; I'm through with
over-production'.

It's no go the gossip column, it's no go the ceilidh,
All we want is a mother's help and a sugar-stick for the baby.

Willie Murray cut his thumb, couldn't count the damage,
Took the hide of an Ayrshire cow and used it for a bandage.
His brother caught three hundred cran when the seas were
lavish,
Threw the bleeders back in the sea and went upon the parish.

It's no go the Herring Board, it's no go the Bible,
All we want is a packet of fags when our hands are idle.

It's no go the picture palace, it's no go the stadium,
It's no go the country cot with a pot of pink geraniums,
It's no go the Government grants, it's no go the elections,
Sit on your arse for fifty years and hang your hat on a pension.

It's no go my honey love, it's no go my poppet;
Work your hands from day to day, the winds will blow the profit.
The glass is falling hour by hour, the glass will fall for ever,
But if you break the bloody glass you won't hold up the weather.

— ∘•∘ —

Louis MacNeice

128

The Listeners

'Is there anybody there?' said the Traveller,
  Knocking on the moonlit door;
And his horse in the silence champed the grasses
  Of the forest's ferny floor:
And a bird flew up out of the turret,
  Above the Traveller's head:
And he smote upon the door again a second time;
  'Is there anybody there?' he said.
But no one descended to the Traveller;
  No head from the leaf-fringed sill
Leaned over and looked into his grey eyes,
  Where he stood perplexed and still.
But only a host of phantom listeners
  That dwelt in the lone house then
Stood listening in the quiet of the moonlight
  To that voice from the world of men:
Stood thronging the faint moonbeams on the dark stair,
  That goes down to the empty hall,
Hearkening in an air stirred and shaken
  By the lonely Traveller's call.
And he felt in his heart their strangeness,
  Their stillness answering his cry,
While his horse moved, cropping the dark turf,
  'Neath the starred and leafy sky;
For he suddenly smote on the door, even
  Louder, and lifted his head: –
'Tell them I came, and no one answered,
  That I kept my word,' he said.
Never the least stir made the listeners,
  Though every word he spake
Fell echoing through the shadowiness of the still house
  From the one man left awake:
Ay, they heard his foot upon the stirrup,
  And the sound of iron on stone,
And how the silence surged softly backward,
  When the plunging hoofs were gone.

WALTER DE LA MARE

The Passionate Shepherd to his Love

Come live with me and be my Love,
And we will all the pleasures prove
That hills and valleys, dale and field,
And all the craggy mountains yield.

There will we sit upon the rocks
And see the shepherds feed their flocks,
By shallow rivers, to whose falls
Melodious birds sing madrigals.

There will I make thee beds of roses
And a thousand fragrant posies,
A cap of flowers, and a kirtle
Embroider'd all with leaves of myrtle.

A gown made of the finest wool,
Which from our pretty lambs we pull,
Fair linèd slippers for the cold,
With buckles of the purest gold.

A belt of straw and ivy buds
With coral clasps and amber studs:
And if these pleasures may thee move,
Come live with me and be my Love.

The shepherd swains shall dance and sing
For thy delight each May-morning:
If these delights thy mind may move,
Then live with me and be my Love.

CHRISTOPHER MARLOWE

To his Coy Mistress

Had we but world enough, and time,
This coyness, lady, were no crime.
We would sit down, and think which way
To walk, and pass our long love's day.
Thou by the Indian Ganges' side
Should'st rubies find: I by the tide
Of Humber would complain. I would
Love you ten years before the Flood,
And you should, if you please, refuse
Till the conversion of the Jews.
My vegetable love should grow
Vaster than empires, and more slow.
An hundred years should go to praise
Thine eyes, and on thy forehead gaze:
Two hundred to adore each breast;
But thirty thousand to the rest;
An age at least to every part,
And the last age should show your heart.
For, lady, you deserve this state,
Nor would I love at lower rate.
   But at my back I always hear
Time's wingèd chariot hurrying near:
And yonder all before us lie
Deserts of vast eternity.
Thy beauty shall no more be found;
Nor, in thy marble vault, shall sound
My echoing song: then worms shall try
That long-preserved virginity,
And your quaint honour turn to dust,
And into ashes all my lust.
The grave's a fine and private place,
But none, I think, do there embrace.
   Now, therefore, while the youthful hue
Sits on thy skin like morning dew,
And while thy willing soul transpires
At every pore with instant fires,
Now let us sport us while we may;
And now, like amorous birds of prey,

Rather at once our Time devour,
Than languish in his slow-chapt power.
Let us roll all our strength and all
Our sweetness up into one ball,
And tear our pleasures with rough strife
Thorough the iron gates of life.
Thus, though we cannot make our Sun
Stand still, yet we will make him run.

—◦◦◦—

ANDREW MARVELL

Sea Fever

I must go down to the seas again, to the lonely sea and the sky,
And all I ask is a tall ship and a star to steer her by,
And the wheel's kick and the wind's song and the white sails
shaking,
And a grey mist on the sea's face and a grey dawn breaking.

I must go down to the seas again, for the call of the running tide
Is a wild call and a clear call that may not be denied;
And all I ask is a windy day with the white clouds flying,
And the flung spray and the blown spume, and the sea-gulls
crying.

I must go down to the seas again, to the vagrant gypsy life,
To the gull's way and the whale's way where the wind's like a
whetted knife;
And all I ask is a merry yarn from a laughing fellow-rover,
And quiet sleep and a sweet dream when the long trick's over.

JOHN MASEFIELD

Cargoes

Quinquireme of Nineveh from distant Ophir
Rowing home to haven in sunny Palestine,
With a cargo of ivory,
And apes and peacocks,
Sandalwood, cedarwood, and sweet white wine.

Stately Spanish galleon coming from the Isthmus,
Dipping through the Tropics by the palm-green shores,
With a cargo of diamonds,
Emeralds, amethysts,
Topazes, and cinnamon, and gold moidores.

Dirty British coaster with a salt-caked smoke stack
Butting through the channel in the mad March days,
With a cargo of Tyne coal,
Road-rail, pig-lead,
Firewood, iron-ware, and cheap tin trays.

JOHN MASEFIELD

My Candle Burns at Both Ends

My candle burns at both ends;
  It will not last the night;
But ah, my foes, and oh, my friends –
  It gives a lovely light!

EDNA ST VINCENT MILLAY

L'Allegro

Hence, loathed Melancholy,
Of Cerberus and blackest Midnight born,
In Stygian cave forlorn,
   'Mongst horrid shapes, and shrieks, and sights unholy!
Find out some uncouth cell,
   Where brooding Darkness spreads his jealous wings,
And the night-raven sings;
   There under ebon shades, and low-brow'd rocks,
As ragged as thy locks,
   In dark Cimmerian desert ever dwell.
   But come, thou goddess fair and free,
In Heaven yclep'd Euphrosyne,
And by men, heart-easing Mirth;
Whom lovely Venus, at a birth,
With two sister Graces more,
To ivy-crownèd Bacchus bore:
Or whether (as some sager sing)
The frolic wind, that breathes the spring,
Zephyr, with Aurora playing,
As he met her once a-maying;
There on beds of violets blue,
And fresh-blown roses wash'd in dew,
Fill'd her with thee, a daughter fair,
So buxom, blithe, and debonair.
   Haste thee, Nymph, and bring with thee
Jest and youthful Jollity,
Quips, and Cranks, and wanton Wiles,
Nods, and Becks, and wreathed Smiles,
Such as hang on Hebe's cheek,
And love to live in dimple sleek;
Sport that wrinkled Care derides,
And Laughter holding both his sides.
Come, and trip it, as you go,
On the light fantastic toe;
And in thy right hand lead with thee
The mountain-nymph, sweet Liberty;
And, if I give thee honour due,
Mirth, admit me of thy crew,

To live with her, and live with thee,
In unreprovèd pleasures free.
To hear the lark begin his flight,
And singing startle the dull Night,
From his watch-tower in the skies,
Till the dappled Dawn doth rise;
Then to come, in spite of sorrow,
And at my window bid good morrow,
Through the sweetbriar, or the vine,
Or the twisted eglantine:
While the cock, with lively din,
Scatters the rear of Darkness thin.
And to the stack, or the barn door,
Stoutly struts his dames before:
Oft listening how the hounds and horn
Cheerly rouse the slumbering Morn,
From the side of some hoar hill,
Through the high wood echoing shrill:
Some time walking, not unseen,
By hedge-row elms, on hillocks green,
Right against the eastern gate
Where the great Sun begins his state,
Robed in flames, and amber light,
The clouds in thousand liveries dight;
While the ploughman, near at hand,
Whistles o'er the furrow'd land,
And the milkmaid singeth blithe,
And the mower whets his scythe,
And every shepherd tells his tale
Under the hawthorn in the dale.
Straight mine eye hath caught new pleasures,
Whilst the landscape round it measures;
Russet lawns, and fallows gray,
Where the nibbling flocks do stray;
Mountains, on whose barren breast
The labouring clouds do often rest;
Meadows trim with daisies pied,
Shallow brooks, and rivers wide:
Towers and battlements it sees
Bosom'd high in tufted trees,
Where perhaps some beauty lies,
The Cynosure of neighbouring eyes.
Hard by, a cottage chimney smokes,

From betwixt two aged oaks,
Where Corydon and Thyrsis, met,
Are at their savoury dinner set
Of herbs and other country messes,
Which the neat-handed Phyllis dresses;
And then in haste her bower she leaves,
With Thestylis to bind the sheaves;
Or, if the earlier season lead,
To the tann'd haycock in the mead.
Sometimes with secure delight
The upland hamlets will invite,
When the merry bells ring round,
And the jocund rebecks sound
To many a youth and many a maid,
Dancing in the chequer'd shade;
And young and old come forth to play
On a sun-shine holiday,
Till the live-long daylight fail:
Then to the spicy nut-brown ale,
With stories told of many a feat,
How faery Mab the junkets eat;
She was pinch'd, and pull'd, she said;
And he, by friar's lantern led,
Tells how the drudging goblin sweat,
To earn his cream-bowl duly set,
When in one night, ere glimpse of morn,
His shadowy flail hath thresh'd the corn,
That ten day-labourers could not end;
Then lies him down the lubber fiend,
And, stretch'd out all the chimney's length,
Basks at the fire his hairy strength;
And crop-full out of doors he flings
Ere the first cock his matin rings.
Thus done the tales, to bed they creep,
By whispering winds soon lull'd asleep.
Tower'd cities please us then,
And the busy hum of men,
Where throngs of knights and barons bold,
In weeds of peace, high triumphs hold,
With store of ladies, whose bright eyes
Rain influence, and judge the prize
Of wit, or arms, while both contend
To win her grace, whom all commend.

There let Hymen oft appear
In saffron robe, with taper clear,
And pomp, and feast, and revelry,
With mask, and antique pageantry;
Such sights as youthful poets dream
On summer eves by haunted stream.
Then to the well-trod stage anon,
If Jonson's learned sock be on,
Or sweetest Shakespeare, Fancy's child,
Warble his native wood-notes wild.
    And ever, against eating cares,
Lap me in soft Lydian airs,
Married to immortal verse;
Such as the meeting soul may pierce,
In notes, with many a winding bout
Of linked sweetness long drawn out,
With wanton heed and giddy cunning;
The melting voice through mazes running,
Untwisting all the chains that tie
The hidden soul of harmony;
That Orpheus' self may heave his head
From golden slumber on a bed
Of heap'd Elysian flowers, and hear
Such strains as would have won the ear
Of Pluto, to have quite set free
His half-regain'd Eurydice.
    These delights if thou canst give,
Mirth, with thee I mean to live.

———◆◆———

JOHN MILTON

On His Blindness

When I consider how my light is spent
Ere half my days, in this dark world and wide,
And that one talent which is death to hide
Lodged with me useless, though my soul more bent

To serve therewith my Maker, and present
My true account, lest He returning chide, –
Doth God exact day-labour, light denied?
I fondly ask: – But Patience, to prevent

That murmur, soon replies; God doth not need
Either man's work, or His own gifts: who best
Bear His mild yoke, they serve Him best: His state

Is kingly; thousands at His bidding speed
And post o'er land and ocean without rest: –
They also serve who only stand and wait.

JOHN MILTON

Oft in the Stilly Night

Oft in the stilly night
  Ere slumber's chain has bound me,
Fond Memory brings the light
  Of other days around me:
    The smiles, the tears
    Of boyhood's years,
  The words of love then spoken;
    The eyes that shone,
    Now dimm'd and gone,
  The cheerful hearts now broken!
Thus in the stilly night
  Ere slumber's chain has bound me,
Sad Memory brings the light
  Of other days around me.

When I remember all
  The friends so link'd together
I've seen around me fall
  Like leaves in wintry weather,
    I feel like one
    Who treads alone
  Some banquet-hall deserted,
    Whose lights are fled
    Whose garlands dead,
  And all but he departed!
Thus in the stilly night
  Ere slumber's chain has bound me,
Sad Memory brings the light
  Of other days around me.

THOMAS MOORE

Vitaï Lampada

There's a breathless hush in the Close to-night –
  Ten to make and the match to win –
A bumping pitch and a blinding light,
  An hour to play and the last man in.
And it's not for the sake of a ribboned coat,
  Or the selfish hope of a season's fame,
But his Captain's hand on his shoulder smote –
  'Play up! play up! and play the game!'

The sand of the desert is sodden red, –
  Red with the wreck of a square that broke; –
The Gatling's jammed and the Colonel dead,
  And the regiment blind with dust and smoke.
The river of death has brimmed his banks,
  And England's far, and Honour a name,
But the voice of a schoolboy rallies the ranks:
  'Play up! play up! and play the game!'

This is the word that year by year,
  While in her place the School is set,
Every one of her sons must hear,
  And none that hears it dare forget.
This they all with a joyful mind
  Bear through life like a torch in flame,
And falling fling to the host behind –
  'Play up! play up! and play the game!'

HENRY NEWBOLT

The Highwayman

The wind was a torrent of darkness among the gusty trees,
The moon was a ghostly galleon tossed upon cloudy seas,
The road was a ribbon of moonlight over the purple moor,
And the highwayman came riding –
  Riding – riding –
The highwayman came riding, up to the old inn-door.

He'd a French cocked-hat on his forehead, a bunch of lace at his
 chin,
A coat of claret velvet, and breeches of brown doe-skin;
They fitted with never a wrinkle: his boots were up to the thigh!
And he rode with a jewelled twinkle,
  His pistol butts a-twinkle,
His rapier hilt a-twinkle, under the jewelled sky.

Over the cobbles he clattered and clashed in the dark inn-yard,
And he tapped with his whip on the shutters, but all was locked
 and barred;
He whistled a tune to the window, and who should be waiting
 there
But the landlord's black-eyed daughter,
  Bess, the landlord's daughter,
Plaiting a dark red love-knot into her long black hair.

And dark in the old inn-yard a stable-wicket creaked
Where Tim the ostler listened; his face was white and peaked;
His eyes were hollows of madness, his hair like mouldy hay,
But he loved the landlord's daughter,
  The landlord's red-lipped daughter;
Dumb as a dog he listened, and he heard the robber say –

'One kiss, my bonny sweetheart, I'm after a prize to-night,
But I shall be back with the yellow gold before the morning light;
Yet, if they press me sharply, and harry me through the day,
Then look for me by moonlight,
  Watch for me by moonlight,
I'll come to thee by moonlight, though hell should bar the way.'

He rose upright in the stirrups; he scarce could reach her hand,
But she loosened her hair i' the casement! His face burnt like a
　　brand
As the black cascade of perfume came tumbling over his breast;
And he kissed its waves in the moonlight,
　　　　(Oh, sweet black waves in the moonlight!)
Then he tugged at his rein in the moonlight, and galloped away to
　　the west.

II

He did not come in the dawning; he did not come at noon;
And out o' the tawny sunset, before the rise o' the moon,
When the road was a gipsy's ribbon, looping the purple moor,
A red-coat troop came marching –
　　　Marching – marching –
King George's men came marching, up to the old inn-door.

They said no word to the landlord, they drank his ale instead,
But they gagged his daughter and bound her to the foot of her
　　narrow bed;
Two of them knelt at her casement, with muskets at their side!
There was death at every window;
　　　And hell at one dark window;
For Bess could see, through her casement, the road that *he* would
　　ride.

They had tied her up to attention, with many a sniggering jest;
They had bound a musket beside her, with the barrel beneath her
　　breast!
'Now keep good watch!' and they kissed her.
　　　She heard the dead man say –
Look for me by moonlight;
　　　Watch for me by moonlight;
I'll come to thee by moonlight, though hell should bar the way!

She twisted her hands behind her; but all the knots held good!
She writhed her hands till her fingers were wet with sweat or
　　blood!
They stretched and strained in the darkness, and the hours
　　crawled by like years,
Till, now, on the stroke of midnight,
　　　Cold, on the stroke of midnight,
The tip of one finger touched it! The trigger at least was hers!

The tip of one finger touched it; she strove no more for the rest!
Up, she stood to attention, with the barrel beneath her breast,
She would not risk their hearing; she would not strive again;
For the road lay bare in the moonlight;
      Blank and bare in the moonlight;
And the blood of her veins in the moonlight throbbed to her
  love's refrain.

Tlot-tlot; tlot-tlot! Had they heard it? The horse-hoofs ringing
  clear;
Tlot-tlot, tlot-tlot, in the distance? Were they deaf that they did not
  hear?
Down the ribbon of moonlight, over the brow of the hill,
The highwayman came riding,
      Riding, riding!
The red-coats looked to their priming! She stood up, straight and
  still!

Tlot-tlot, in the frosty silence! *tlot-tlot,* in the echoing night!
Nearer he came and nearer! Her face was like a light!
Her eyes grew wide for a moment; she drew one last deep breath,
Then her finger moved in the moonlight,
      Her musket shattered the moonlight,
Shattered her breast in the moonlight and warned him – with her
  death.

He turned; he spurred to the westward; he did not know who
  stood
Bowed, with her head o'er the musket, drenched with her own
  red blood!
Not till the dawn he heard it, and slowly blanched to hear
How Bess, the landlord's daughter,
      The landlord's black-eyed daughter,
Had watched for her love in the moonlight, and died in the
  darkness there.

Back, he spurred like a madman, shrieking a curse to the sky,
With the white road smoking behind him and his rapier
  brandished high!
Blood-red were his spurs i' the golden noon; wine-red was his
  velvet coat;
When they shot him down on the highway,
      Down like a dog on the highway,
And he lay in his blood on the highway, with the bunch of lace at
  his throat.

And still of a winter's night, they say, when the wind is in the trees,
When the moon is a ghostly galleon tossed upon cloudy seas,
When the road is a ribbon of moonlight over the purple moor,
A highwayman comes riding –
        Riding – riding –
A highwayman comes riding, up to the old inn-door.

Over the cobbles he clatters and clangs in the dark inn-yard
And he taps with his whip on the shutters, but all is locked and barred;
He whistles a tune to the window, and who should be waiting there
But the landlord's black-eyed daughter,
        Bess, the landlord's daughter,
Plaiting a dark red love-knot into her long black hair.

———◦◦———

ALFRED NOYES

Ode

We are the music makers,
  And we are the dreamers of dreams,
Wandering by lone sea-breakers,
  And sitting by desolate streams; –
World-losers and world-forsakers,
  On whom the pale moon gleams:
Yet we are the movers and shakers
  Of the world for ever, it seems.

With wonderful deathless ditties
We build up the world's great cities,
  And out of a fabulous story
  We fashion an empire's glory:
One man with a dream, at pleasure,
  Shall go forth and conquer a crown;
And three with a new song's measure
  Can trample a kingdom down.

We, in the ages lying
  In the buried past of the earth,
Built Nineveh with our sighing,
  And Babel itself in our mirth;
And o'erthrew them with prophesying
  To the old of the new world's worth;
For each age is a dream that is dying,
  Or one that is coming to birth.

A breath of our inspiration
Is the life of each generation;
  A wondrous thing of our dreaming
  Unearthly, impossible seeming –
The soldier, the king, and the peasant
  Are working together in one,
Till our dream shall become their present,
  And their work in the world be done.

They had no vision amazing
Of the goodly house they are raising;
  They had no divine foreshowing
  Of the land to which they are going:
But on one man's soul it hath broken,
  A light that doth not depart;
And his look, or a word he hath spoken,
  Wrought flame in another man's heart.

And therefore to-day is thrilling
With a past day's late fulfilling;
  And the multitudes are enlisted
  In the faith that their fathers resisted,
And, scorning the dream of to-morrow,
  Are bringing to pass, as they may,
In the world, for its joy or its sorrow,
  The dream that was scorned yesterday.

But we, with our dreaming and singing,
  Ceaseless and sorrowless we!
The glory about us clinging
  Of the glorious futures we see,
Our souls with high music ringing:
  O men! it must ever be
That we dwell, in our dreaming and singing,
  A little apart from ye.

For we are afar with the dawning
  And the suns that are not yet high,
And out of the infinite morning
  Intrepid you hear us cry –
How, spite of your human scorning,
  Once more God's future draws nigh,
And already goes forth the warning
  That ye of the past must die.

Great hail! we cry to the comers
  From the dazzling unknown shore;
Bring us hither your sun and your summers,
  And renew our world as of yore;
You shall teach us your song's new numbers,
  And things that we dreamed not before:
Yea, in spite of a dreamer who slumbers,
  And a singer who sings no more.

———◆◇◆———

ARTHUR O'SHAUGHNESSY

Anthem for Doomed Youth

What passing-bells for these who die as cattle?
 Only the monstrous anger of the guns.
Only the stuttering rifles' rapid rattle
 Can patter out their hasty orisons.
No mockeries now for them; no prayers nor bells,
 Nor any voice of mourning save the choirs, –
The shrill, demented choirs of wailing shells;
 And bugles calling for them from sad shires.

What candles may be held to speed them all?
 Not in the hands of boys, but in their eyes
 Shall shine the holy glimmers of good-byes.
The pallor of girls' brows shall be their pall;
 Their flowers the tenderness of patient minds,
 And each slow dusk a drawing-down of blinds.

WILFRED OWEN

Futility

Move him into the sun –
Gently its touch awoke him once,
At home, whispering of fields unsown.
Always it woke him, even in France,
Until this morning and this snow.
If anything might rouse him now
The kind old sun will know.

Think how it wakes the seeds, –
Woke, once, the clays of a cold star.
Are limbs, so dear-achieved, are sides,
Full-nerved, – still warm, – too hard to stir?
Was it for this the clay grew tall?
– O what made fatuous sunbeams toil
To break earth's sleep at all?

WILFRED OWEN

The Man from Snowy River

There was movement at the station, for the word had passed
around
That the colt from old Regret had got away,
And had joined the wild bush horses – he was worth a thousand
pound,
So all the cracks had gathered to the fray.
All the tried and noted riders from the stations near and far
Had mustered at the homestead overnight,
For the bushmen love hard riding where the wild bush horses
are,
And the stock-horse snuffs the battle with delight.

There was Harrison, who made his pile when Pardon won the
cup,
The old man with his hair as white as snow;
But few could ride beside him when his blood was fairly up –
He would go wherever horse and man could go.
And Clancy of the Overflow came down to lend a hand,
No better horseman ever held the reins;
For never horse could throw him while the saddle-girths would
stand –
He learnt to ride while droving on the plains.

And one was there, a stripling on a small and weedy beast;
He was something like a racehorse undersized,
With a touch of Timor pony – three parts thoroughbred at least –
And such as are by mountain horsemen prized.
He was hard and tough and wiry – just the sort that won't say die –
There was courage in his quick impatient tread;
And he bore the badge of gameness in his bright and fiery eye,
And the proud and lofty carriage of his head.

But still so slight and weedy, one would doubt his power to stay,
And the old man said, 'That horse will never do
For a long and tiring gallop – lad, you'd better stop away,
Those hills are far too rough for such as you.'
So he waited, sad and wistful – only Clancy stood his friend –
'I think we ought to let him come,' he said;
'I warrant he'll be with us when he's wanted at the end,
For both his horse and he are mountain bred.

'He hails from Snowy River, up by Kosciusko's side,
Where the hills are twice as steep and twice as rough;
Where a horse's hoofs strike firelight from the flint stones every
     stride,
The man that holds his own is good enough.
And the Snowy River riders on the mountains make their home,
Where the river runs those giant hills between;
I have seen full many horsemen since I first commenced to roam,
But nowhere yet such horsemen have I seen.'

So he went; they found the horses by the big mimosa clump,
They raced away towards the mountain's brow,
And the old man gave his orders, 'Boys, go at them from the
     jump,
No use to try for fancy riding now.
And, Clancy, you must wheel them, try and wheel them to the
     right.
Ride boldly, lad, and never fear the spills,
For never yet was rider that could keep the mob in sight,
If once they gain the shelter of those hills.'

So Clancy rode to wheel them – he was racing on the wing
Where the best and boldest riders take their place,
And he raced his stock-horse past them, and he made the ranges
     ring
With the stockwhip, as he met them face to face.
Then they halted for a moment, while he swung the dreaded
     lash,
But they saw their well-loved mountain full in view,
And they charged beneath the stockwhip with a sharp and
     sudden dash,
And off into the mountain scrub they flew.

Then fast the horsemen followed, where the gorges deep and
    black
  Resounded to the thunder of their tread,
And the stockwhips woke the echoes, and they fiercely answered
    back
  From cliffs and crags that beetled overhead.
And upward, ever upward, the wild horses held their way,
  Where mountain ash and kurrajong grew wide;
And the old man muttered fiercely, 'We may bid the mob good
    day,
  No man can hold them down the other side.'

When they reached the mountain's summit, even Clancy took a
    pull –
  It well might make the boldest hold their breath ;
The wild hop scrub grew thickly, and the hidden ground was full
  Of wombat holes, and any slip was death.
But the man from Snowy River let the pony have his head,
  And he swung his stockwhip round and gave a cheer,
And he raced him down the mountain like a torrent down its bed,
  While the others stood and watched in very fear.

He sent the flint-stones flying, but the pony kept his feet,
  He cleared the fallen timber in his stride,
And the man from Snowy River never shifted in his seat –
  It was grand to see that mountain horseman ride.
Through the stringy barks and saplings, on the rough and broken
    ground,
  Down the hillside at a racing pace he went;
And he never drew the bridle till he landed safe and sound
  At the bottom of that terrible descent.

He was right among the horses as they climbed the farther hill,
  And the watchers on the mountain, standing mute,
Saw him ply the stockwhip fiercely; he was right among them
    still,
  As he raced across the clearing in pursuit.
Then they lost him for a moment, where two mountain gullies
    met
  In the ranges – but a final glimpse reveals
On a dim and distant hillside the wild horses racing yet,
  With the man from Snowy River at their heels.

And he ran them single-handed till their sides were white with
    foam;
    He followed like a bloodhound on their track,
Till they halted, cowed and beaten; then he turned their heads for
    home,
    And alone and unassisted brought them back.
But his hardy mountain pony he could scarcely raise a trot,
    He was blood from hip to shoulder from the spur;
But his pluck was still undaunted, and his courage fiery hot,
    For never yet was mountain horse a cur.

And down by Kosciusko, where the pine-clad ridges raise
    Their torn and rugged battlements on high,
Where the air is clear as crystal, and the white stars fairly blaze
    At midnight in the cold and frosty sky,
And where around the Overflow the reed-beds sweep and sway
    To the breezes, and the rolling plains are wide,
The Man from Snowy River is a household word today,
    And the stockmen tell the story of his ride.

———◦◦———

A. B. 'BANJO' PATERSON

The Raven

Once upon a midnight dreary, while I pondered, weak and
  weary,
Over many a quaint and curious volume of forgotten lore –
While I nodded, nearly napping, suddenly there came a tapping,
As of some one gently rapping, rapping at my chamber door –
''Tis some visitor,' I muttered, 'tapping at my chamber door –
      Only this, and nothing more.'

Ah! distinctly I remember, it was in the bleak December,
And each separate dying ember wrought its ghost upon the floor,
Eagerly I wished the morrow; vainly I had sought to borrow
From my books surcease of sorrow – sorrow for the lost Lenore –
For the rare and radiant maiden, whom the angels named Lenore –
      Nameless here for evermore.

And the silken, sad, uncertain rustling of each purple curtain
Thrilled me – filled me with fantastic terrors never felt before;
So that now, to still the beating of my heart, I stood repeating,
''Tis some visitor entreating entrance at my chamber door –
Some late visitor entreating entrance at my chamber door:
      This it is, and nothing more.'

Presently my soul grew stronger; hesitating then no longer,
'Sir,' said I, 'or madam, truly your forgiveness I implore;
But the fact is, I was napping, and so gently you came rapping,
And so faintly you came tapping, tapping at my chamber door,
That I scarce was sure I heard you.' Here I opened wide the door:
      Darkness there, and nothing more.

Deep into that darkness peering, long I stood there, wondering,
  fearing,
Doubting, dreaming dreams no mortal ever dared to dream
  before;
But the silence was unbroken, and the stillness gave no token,
And the only word there spoken was the whispered word
  'Lenore!'
This I whispered, and an echo murmured back the word 'Lenore!'
      Merely this, and nothing more.

Back into my chamber turning, all my soul within me burning,
Soon again I heard a tapping, something louder than before:
'Surely,' said I, 'surely that is something at my window lattice;
Let me see then what thereat is, and this mystery explore –
Let my heart be still a moment, and this mystery explore.
 'Tis the wind, and nothing more.'

Open here I flung the shutter, when, with many a flirt and flutter,
In there stepped a stately Raven, of the saintly days of yore;
Not the least obeisance made he, not a minute stopped or stayed
 he;
But with mien of lord or lady perched above my chamber door –
Perched above a bust of Pallas, just above my chamber door –
 Perched, and sat, and nothing more.

Then this ebony bird beguiling my sad fancy into smiling,
By the grave and stern decorum of the countenance it wore:
'Though thy crest be shorn and shaven, thou,' I said, 'art sure no
 craven;
Ghastly, grim, and ancient Raven, wandering from the nightly
 shore,
Tell me what thy lordly name is on the night's Plutonian shore?'
 Quoth the Raven, 'Never more.'

Much I marvelled this ungainly fowl to hear discourse so plainly,
Though its answer little meaning, little relevancy bore;
For we cannot help agreeing that no living human being
Ever yet was blessed with seeing bird above his chamber door –
Bird or beast upon the sculptured bust above his chamber door
 With such name as 'Never more.'

But the Raven, sitting lonely on that placid bust, spoke only
That one word, as if his soul in that one word he did outpour;
Nothing further then he uttered, not a feather then he fluttered,
Till I scarcely more than muttered – 'Other friends have flown
 before,
On the morrow *he* will leave me, as my hopes have flown before.'
 Then the bird said, 'Never more.'

Startled by the stillness broken by reply so aptly spoken,
'Doubtless,' said I, 'what it utters is its only stock and store,
Caught from some unhappy master, whom unmerciful disaster
Followed fast and followed faster, till his songs one burden bore –
Till the dirges of his hope this melancholy burden bore –
      Of "Never, never more."'

But the raven still beguiling all my sad soul into smiling,
Straight I wheeled a cushioned seat in front of bird, and bust, and
    door;
Then upon the velvet sinking, I betook myself to linking
Fancy into fancy, thinking what this ominous bird of yore –
What this grim, ungainly, ghastly, gaunt, and ominous bird of
    yore
      Meant in croaking 'Never more.'

Thus I sat engaged in guessing, but no syllable expressing
To the fowl whose fiery eyes now burned into my bosom's core;
This and more I sat divining, with my head at ease reclining
On the cushion's velvet lining, that the lamp-light gloated o'er,
But whose violet velvet lining, with the lamp-light gloating o'er,
      She shall press – ah, never more!

Then methought the air grew denser, perfumed from an unseen
    censer
Swung by seraphim, whose footfalls tinkled on the tufted floor.
'Wretch,' I cried, 'thy God hath lent thee – by these angels He
    hath sent thee
Respite – respite and nepenthe from my memories of Lenore!
Quaff – oh, quaff this kind nepenthe, and forget this lost Lenore!'
      Quoth the Raven, 'Never more.'

'Prophet,' said I, 'thing of evil! – prophet still, if bird or devil!
Whether tempter sent, or whether tempest tossed thee here
    ashore
Desolate, yet all undaunted, on this desert land enchanted,
On this home by horror haunted – tell me truly, I implore,
Is there – *is* there balm in Gilead? – tell me, tell me, I implore!'
      Quoth the Raven, 'Never more.'

'Prophet,' said I, 'thing of evil! – prophet still, if bird or devil!
By that heaven that bends above us – by that God we both adore –
Tell this soul, with sorrow laden, if, within the distant Aidenn,
It shall clasp a sainted maiden, whom the angels name Lenore! –
Clasp a rare and radiant maiden, whom the angels name Lenore?'
        Quoth the Raven, 'Never more.'

'Be that word our sign of parting, bird of fiend,' I shrieked,
        upstarting –
'Get thee back into the tempest and the night's Plutonian shore;
Leave no black plume as a token of that lie thy soul hath spoken,
Leave my loneliness unbroken – quit the bust above my door,
Take thy beak from out my heart, and take thy form from off my
        door!'
        Quoth the Raven, 'Never more.'

And the Raven, never flitting, still is sitting, still is sitting,
On the pallid bust of Pallas, just above my chamber door;
And his eyes have all the seeming of a demon's that is dreaming,
And the lamp-light o'er him streaming throws his shadow on the
        floor;
And my soul from out that shadow that lies floating on the floor
        Shall be lifted – never more!

—◦—

EDGAR ALLAN POE

The Dying Christian to his Soul

Vital spark of heavenly flame,
Quit, oh quit this mortal frame:
Trembling, hoping, lingering, flying –
Oh the pain, the bliss of dying!
Cease, fond Nature, cease thy strife,
And let me languish into life!

Hark! they whisper; angels say,
Sister spirit, come away!
What is this absorbs me quite?
Steals my senses, shuts my sight,
Drowns my spirits, draws my breath?
Tell me, my soul, can this be death?

The world recedes; it disappears!
Heaven opens on my eyes! my ears
With sounds seraphic ring:
Lend, lend your wings: I mount! I fly!
O Grave! where is thy victory?
O Death! where is thy sting?

ALEXANDER POPE

from *An Essay on Criticism*

A little learning is a dang'rous thing;
Drink deep, or taste not the Pierian spring:
There shallow draughts intoxicate the brain,
And drinking largely sobers us again.

*   *   *

Hope springs eternal in the human breast;
Man never is, but always to be blessed.
The soul, uneasy, and confined from home,
Rests and expatiates in a life to come.

ALEXANDER POPE

For Johnny

Do not despair
For Johnny-head-in-air;
He sleeps as sound
As Johnny under ground.

Fetch out no shroud
For Johnny-in-the-cloud;
And keep your tears
For him in after years.

Better by far
For Johnny-the-bright-star,
To keep your head,
And see his children fed.

JOHN PUDNEY

Song

When I am dead, my dearest,
Sing no sad songs for me;
Plant thou no roses at my head,
Nor shady cypress tree:
Be the green grass above me
With showers and dewdrops wet;
And if thou wilt, remember,
And if thou wilt, forget.

I shall not see the shadows,
I shall not feel the rain;
I shall not hear the nightingale
Sing on, as if in pain;
And dreaming through the twilight
That doth not rise nor set,
Haply I may remember,
And haply may forget.

CHRISTINA ROSSETTI

Everyone Sang

Everyone suddenly burst out singing;
And I was filled with such delight
As prisoned birds must find in freedom
Winging wildly across the white
Orchards and dark-green fields; on; on; and out
  of sight.

Everyone's voice was suddenly lifted,
And beauty came like the setting sun.
My heart was shaken with tears; and horror
Drifted away . . . O but every one
Was a bird; and the song was wordless; the singing
  will never be done.

SIEGFRIED SASSOON

from *The Lay of the Last Minstrel*

Breathes there the man, with soul so dead,
Who never to himself hath said,
This is my own, my native land!
Whose heart hath ne'er within him burned,
As home his footsteps he hath turned,
From wandering on a foreign strand!
If such there breathe, go, mark him well;
For him no Minstrel raptures swell;
High though his titles, proud his name,
Boundless his wealth as wish can claim;
Despite those titles, power, and pelf,
The wretch, concentred all in self,
Living, shall forfeit fair renown,
And, doubly dying, shall go down
To the vile dust, from whence he sprung,
Unwept, unhonoured, and unsung.

SIR WALTER SCOTT

from *Marmion: Young Lochinvar*

Oh, young Lochinvar is come out of the west,
Through all the wide Border his steed was the best;
And save his good broad-sword he weapon had none,
He rode all unarm'd, and he rode all alone!
So faithful in love, and so dauntless in war,
There never was knight like the young Lochinvar!

He stay'd not for brake, and he stopp'd not for stone,
He swam the Esk river where ford there was none –
But, ere he alighted at Netherby gate,
The bride had consented, the gallant came late:
For a laggard in love, and a dastard in war,
Was to wed the fair Ellen of brave Lochinvar.

So boldly he enter'd the Netherby Hall,
'Mong bride's-men, and kinsmen, and brothers, and all!
Then spoke the bride's father, his hand on his sword –
For the poor craven bridegroom said never a word –
'O come ye in peace here, or come ye in war?
Or to dance at our bridal? young Lord Lochinvar!

'I long woo'd your daughter, my suit you denied:
Love swells like the Solway, but ebbs like its tide!
And now am I come, with this lost love of mine,
To lead but one measure, drink one cup of wine!
There be maidens in Scotland, more lovely by far,
That would gladly be bride to the young Lochinvar!'

The bride kiss'd the goblet; the knight took it up,
He quaff'd off the wine, and he threw down the cup!
She look'd down to blush, and she look'd up to sigh,
With a smile on her lips and a tear in her eye.
He took her soft hand, ere her mother could bar –
'Now tread we a measure!' said young Lochinvar.

So stately his form, and so lovely her face,
That never a hall such a galliard did grace!
While her mother did fret, and her father did fume,
And the bridegroom stood dangling his bonnet and plume,
And the bride-maidens whisper'd, "Twere better by far
To have match'd our fair cousin with young Lochinvar!'

One touch to her hand, and one word in her ear,
When they reach'd the hall door, and the charger stood near,
So light to the croupe the fair lady he swung,
So light to the saddle before her he sprung!
'She is won! we are gone, over bank, bush, and scaur;
They'll have fleet steeds that follow!' quoth young Lochinvar.

There was mounting 'mong Græmes of the Netherby clan ;
Fosters, Fenwicks, and Musgraves, they rode and they ran;
There was racing and chasing on Cannobie Lea,
But the lost bride of Netherby ne'er did they see!
So daring in love, and so dauntless in war,
Have ye e'er heard of gallant like young Lochinvar?

SIR WALTER SCOTT

I Have a Rendezvous with Death

I have a rendezvous with Death
At some disputed barricade,
When Spring comes back with rustling shade
And apple-blossoms fill the air –
I have a rendezvous with Death
When Spring brings back blue days and fair.

It may be he shall take my hand
And lead me into his dark land
And close my eyes and quench my breath –
It may be I shall pass him still.
I have a rendezvous with Death
On some scarred slope of battered hill,
When Spring comes round again this year
And the first meadow-flowers appear.

God knows 'twere better to be deep
Pillowed in silk and scented down,
Where love throbs out in blissful sleep,
Pulse nigh to pulse, and breath to breath.
Where hushed awakenings are dear . . .
But I've a rendezvous with Death
At midnight in some flaming town,
When Spring trips north again this year,
And I to my pledged word am true,
I shall not fail that rendezvous.

ALAN SEEGER

Song from *As You Like It*

It was a lover and his lass,
   With a hey, and a ho, and a hey nonino,
That o'er the green corn-field did pass,
   In spring time, the only pretty ring time,
When birds do sing, hey ding a ding, ding;
Sweet lovers love the spring.

Between the acres of the rye,
   With a hey, and a ho, and a hey nonino,
Those pretty country folks would lie,
   In spring time, the only pretty ring time,
When birds do sing, hey ding a ding, ding;
Sweet lovers love the spring.

This carol they began that hour,
   With a hey, and a ho, and a hey nonino,
How that a life was but a flower
   In spring time, the only pretty ring time,
When birds do sing, hey ding a ding, ding;
Sweet lovers love the spring.

And therefore take the present time,
   With a hey, and a ho, and a hey nonino;
For love is crownèd with the prime
   In spring time, the only pretty ring time,
When birds do sing, hey ding a ding, ding;
Sweet lovers love the spring.

WILLIAM SHAKESPEARE

Song from *Much Ado About Nothing*

Sigh no more, ladies, sigh no more,
  Men were deceivers ever;
One foot in sea, and one on shore,
To one thing constant never.
     Then sigh not so,
     But let them go,
  And be you blithe and bonny,
Converting all your sounds of woe
  Into Hey nonny, nonny.

Sing no more ditties, sing no more
  Of dumps so dull and heavy;
The fraud of men was ever so,
  Since summer first was leavy
     Then sigh not so,
     But let them go,
  And be you blithe and bonny,
Converting all your sounds of woe
  Into Hey nonny, nonny!

WILLIAM SHAKESPEARE

Songs from *The Tempest*

Full fathom five thy father lies:
  Of his bones are coral made;
Those are pearls that were his eyes:
  Nothing of him that doth fade,
But doth suffer a sea-change
Into something rich and strange.
Sea-nymphs hourly ring his knell:
Hark! now I hear them, –
  Ding, dong, bell.

*   *   *

Where the bee sucks, there suck I,
In a cowslip's bell I lie,
There I couch when owls do cry,
On the bat's back I do fly
After summer merrily.
  Merrily, merrily, shall I live now
  Under the blossom that hangs on the bough.

WILLIAM SHAKESPEARE

Song from *Twelfth Night*

O mistress mine! where are you roaming,
O! stay and hear; your true love's coming,
  That can sing both high and low.
Trip no further, pretty sweeting;
Journeys end in lovers meeting,
  Every wise man's son doth know.

What is love? 'tis not hereafter;
Present mirth hath present laughter;
  What's to come is still unsure:
In delay there lies no plenty;
Then come kiss me, sweet and twenty,
  Youth's a stuff will not endure.

WILLIAM SHAKESPEARE

Sonnet 18

Shall I compare thee to a summer's day?
Thou art more lovely and more temperate.
Rough winds do shake the darling buds of May,
And summer's lease hath all too short a date.
Sometime too hot the eye of heaven shines,
And often is his gold complexion dimmed;
And every fair from fair sometime declines,
By chance, or nature's changing course, untrimmed;
But thy eternal summer shall not fade,
Nor lose possession of that fair thou ow'st,
Nor shall Death brag thou wand'rest in his shade,
When in eternal lines to time thou grow'st.
   So long as men can breathe or eyes can see,
   So long lives this, and this gives life to thee.

WILLIAM SHAKESPEARE

Sonnet 29

When, in disgrace with Fortune and men's eyes,
I all alone beweep my outcast state,
And trouble deaf heaven with my bootless cries,
And look upon myself and curse my fate,
Wishing me like to one more rich in hope,
Featured like him, like him with friends possessed,
Desiring this man's art, and that man's scope,
With what I most enjoy contented least;
Yet in these thoughts myself almost despising,
Haply I think on thee, and then my state,
Like to the lark at break of day arising
From sullen earth, sings hymns at heaven's gate;
    For thy sweet love remember'd such wealth brings,
    That then I scorn to change my state with kings.

WILLIAM SHAKESPEARE

Sonnet 116

Let me not to the marriage of true minds
Admit impediments; love is not love
Which alters when it alteration finds,
Or bends with the remover to remove.
O, no, it is an ever-fixèd mark
That looks on tempests and is never shaken;
It is the star to every wand'ring bark,
Whose worth's unknown, although his height be
    taken.
Love's not Time's fool, though rosy lips and cheeks,
Within his bending sickle's compass come;
Love alters not with his brief hours and weeks,
But bears it out even to the edge of doom.
    If this be error and upon me proved,
    I never writ, nor no man ever loved.

WILLIAM SHAKESPEARE

Music, When Soft Voices Die

Music, when soft voices die,
Vibrates in the memory –
Odours, when sweet violets sicken,
Live within the sense they quicken.

Rose leaves, when the rose is dead,
Are heap'd for the beloved's bed;
And so thy thoughts, when thou art gone,
Love itself shall slumber on.

PERCY BYSSHE SHELLEY

To a Skylark

Hail to thee, blithe Spirit!
  Bird thou never wert,
That from heaven, or near it
  Pourest thy full heart
In profuse strains of unpremeditated art.

Higher still and higher
  From the earth thou springest
Like a cloud of fire;
  The blue deep thou wingest,
And singing still dost soar, and soaring ever singest.

In the golden lightning
  Of the sunken sun
O'er which clouds are brightening,
  Thou dost float and run,
Like an unbodied joy whose race is just begun.

The pale purple even
  Melts around thy flight;
Like a star of heaven
  In the broad daylight
Thou art unseen, but yet I hear thy shrill delight:

Keen as are the arrows
  Of that silver sphere,
Whose intense lamp narrows
  In the white dawn clear
Until we hardly see, we feel that it is there.

All the earth and air
  With thy voice is loud,
As, when night is bare,
  From one lonely cloud
The moon rains out her beams, and heaven is overflow'd.

What thou art we know not;
　　What is most like thee?
From rainbow clouds there flow not
　　Drops so bright to see
As from thy presence showers a rain of melody.

Like a poet hidden
　　In the light of thought,
Singing hymns unbidden,
　　Till the world is wrought
To sympathy with hopes and fears it heeded not:

Like a high-born maiden
　　In a palace tower,
Soothing her love-laden
　　Soul in secret hour
With music sweet as love, which overflows her bower:

Like a glow-worm golden
　　In a dell of dew,
Scattering unbeholden
　　Its aerial hue
Among the flowers and grass, which screen it from the view:

Like a rose embower'd
　　In its own green leaves,
By warm winds deflower'd,
　　Till the scent it gives
Makes faint with too much sweet these heavy-wingèd thieves.

Sound of vernal showers
　　On the twinkling grass,
Rain-awaken'd flowers,
　　All that ever was
Joyous, and clear, and fresh, thy music doth surpass.

Teach us, sprite or bird,
　　What sweet thoughts are thine:
I have never heard
　　Praise of love or wine
That panted forth a flood of rapture so divine.

Chorus hymeneal
    Or triumphal chaunt
Match'd with thine, would be all
    But an empty vaunt –
A thing wherein we feel there is some hidden want.

    What objects are the fountains
        Of thy happy strain?
    What fields, or waves, or mountains?
        What shapes of sky or plain?
What love of thine own kind? what ignorance of pain?

    With thy clear keen joyance
        Languor cannot be:
    Shadow of annoyance
        Never came near thee:
Thou lovest; but ne'er knew love's sad satiety.

    Waking or asleep
        Thou of death must deem
    Things more true and deep
        Than we mortals dream,
Or how could thy notes flow in such a crystal stream?

    We look before and after,
        And pine for what is not:
    Our sincerest laughter
        With some pain is fraught;
Our sweetest songs are those that tell of saddest thought.

    Yet if we could scorn
        Hate, and pride, and fear;
    If we were things born
        Not to shed a tear,
I know not how thy joy we ever should come near.

    Better than all measures
        Of delightful sound,
    Better than all treasures
        That in books are found,
Thy skill to poet were, thou scorner of the ground!

Teach me half the gladness
That thy brain must know,
Such harmonious madness
From my lips would flow
The world should listen then, as I am listening now!

———◦◦◦———

Percy Bysshe Shelley

Ozymandias

I met a traveller from an antique land
Who said: Two vast and trunkless legs of stone
Stand in the desert. Near them on the sand,
Half sunk, a shatter'd visage lies, whose frown
And wrinkled lip and sneer of cold command
Tell that its sculptor well those passions read
Which yet survive, stamp'd on these lifeless things,
The hand that mock'd them and the heart that fed;
And on the pedestal these words appear:
'My name is Ozymandias, king of kings:
Look on my works, ye Mighty, and despair!'
Nothing beside remains. Round the decay
Of that colossal wreck, boundless and bare,
The lone and level sands stretch far away.

PERCY BYSSHE SHELLEY

Ode to the West Wind

O wild West Wind, thou breath of Autumn's being,
Thou, from whose unseen presence the leaves dead
Are driven, like ghosts from an enchanter fleeing,
Yellow, and black, and pale, and hectic red,
Pestilence-stricken multitudes: O thou
Who chariotest to their dark wintry bed
The wingèd seeds, where they lie cold and low,
Each like a corpse within its grave, until
Thine azure sister of the spring shall blow
Her clarion o'er the dreaming earth, and fill
(Driving sweet buds like flocks to feed in air)
With living hues and odours plain and hill:
Wild Spirit, which art moving everywhere;
Destroyer and Preserver; Hear, O hear!

Thou on whose stream, 'mid the steep sky's commotion,
Loose clouds like earth's decaying leaves are shed
Shook from the tangled boughs of Heaven and Ocean,
Angels of rain and lightning; there are spread
On the blue surface of thine airy surge,
Like the bright hair uplifted from the head
Of some fierce Maenad, even from the dim verge
Of the horizon to the zenith's height –
The locks of the approaching storm. Thou dirge
Of the dying year, to which this closing night
Will be the dome of a vast sepulchre,
Vaulted with all thy congregated might
Of vapours, from whose solid atmosphere
Black rain, and fire, and hail, will burst: O hear!

Thou who didst waken from his summer-dreams
The blue Mediterranean, where he lay
Lull'd by the coil of his crystalline streams
Beside a pumice isle in Baiae's bay,
And saw in sleep old palaces and towers
Quivering within the wave's intenser day,
All overgrown with azure moss and flowers
So sweet, the sense faints picturing them! Thou

For whose path the Atlantic's level powers
Cleave themselves into chasms, while far below
The sea-blooms and the oozy woods which wear
The sapless foliage of the ocean, know
Thy voice, and suddenly grow gray with fear
And tremble and despoil themselves: O hear!

If I were a dead leaf thou mightest bear;
If I were a swift cloud to fly with thee;
A wave to pant beneath thy power, and share
The impulse of thy strength, only less free
Than Thou, O uncontrollable! If even
I were as in my boyhood, and could be
The comrade of thy wanderings over heaven,
As then, when to outstrip the skyey speed
Scarce seem'd a vision, I would ne'er have striven
As thus with thee in prayer in my sore need.
O lift me as a wave, a leaf, a cloud!
I fall upon the thorns of life! I bleed!
A heavy weight of hours has chain'd and bow'd
One too like thee: tameless, and swift, and proud.

Make me thy lyre, even as the forest is:
What if my leaves are falling like its own!
The tumult of thy mighty harmonies
Will take from both a deep autumnal tone,
Sweet though in sadness. Be thou, Spirit fierce,
My spirit! be thou me, impetuous one!
Drive my dead thoughts over the universe
Like wither'd leaves to quicken a new birth;
And, by the incantation of this verse,
Scatter, as from an unextinguish'd hearth
Ashes and sparks, my words among mankind!
Be through my lips to unawaken'd earth
The trumpet of a prophecy! O Wind,
If Winter comes, can Spring be far behind?

————•◦•————

PERCY BYSSHE SHELLEY

183

The Bargain

My true love hath my heart, and I have his,
  By just exchange, one for the other given.
I hold his dear, and mine he cannot miss,
  There never was a better bargain driven.
His heart in me keeps me and him in one,
  My heart in him his thoughts and senses guides;
He loves my heart, for once it was his own,
  I cherish his, because in me it bides.
His heart his wound receivèd from my sight,
  My heart was wounded with his wounded heart;
For as from me on him his hurt did light,
  So still methought in me his hurt did smart.
    Both equal hurt, in this change sought our bliss:
    My true love hath my heart and I have his.

SIR PHILIP SIDNEY

For I will Consider my Cat Jeoffry
(from *Jubilate Agno*)

For I will consider my Cat Jeoffry.

For he is the servant of the Living God, duly and daily serving him.

For at the first glance of the glory of God in the East he worships in his way.

For is this done by wreathing his body seven times round with elegant quickness.

For then he leaps up to catch the musk, which is the blessing of God upon his prayer.

For he rolls upon prank to work it in.

For having done duty and received blessing he begins to consider himself.

For this he performs in ten degrees.

For first he looks upon his fore-paws to see if they are clean.

For secondly he kicks up behind to clear away there.

For thirdly he works it upon stretch with the fore paws extended.

For fourthly he sharpens his paws by wood.

For fifthly he washes himself.

For sixthly he rolls upon wash.

For seventhly he fleas himself, that he may not be interrupted upon the beat.

For eighthly he rubs himself against a post.

For ninthly he looks up for his instructions.

For tenthly he goes in quest of food.

For having consider'd God and himself he will consider his neighbour.

For if he meets another cat he will kiss her in kindness.

For when he takes his prey he plays with it to give it chance.

For one mouse in seven escapes by his dallying.

For when his day's work is done his business more properly begins.

For [he] keeps the Lord's watch in the night against the adversary.

For he counteracts the powers of darkness by his electrical skin and glaring eyes.

For he counteracts the Devil, who is death, by brisking about the life.

For in his morning orisons he loves the sun and the sun loves
him.

For he is of the tribe of Tiger.

For the Cherub Cat is a term of the Angel Tiger.

For he has the subtlety and hissing of a serpent, which in
goodness he suppresses.

For he will not do destruction, if he is well-fed, neither will he spit
without provocation.

For he purrs in thankfulness, when God tells him he's a good Cat.

For he is an instrument for the children to learn benevolence
upon.

For every house is incompleat without him and a blessing is
lacking in the spirit.

For the Lord commanded Moses concerning the cats at the
departure of the Children of Israel from Egypt.

For every family had one cat at least in the bag.

For the English Cats are the best in Europe.

For he is the cleanest in the use of his fore-paws of any
quadrupede.

For the dexterity of his defence is an instance of the love of God to
him exceedingly.

For he is the quickest to his mark of any creature.

For he is tenacious of his point.

For he is a mixture of gravity and waggery.

For he knows that God is his Saviour.

For there is nothing sweeter than his peace when at rest.

For there is nothing brisker than his life when in motion.

For he is of the Lord's poor and so indeed is he called by
benevolence perpetually – Poor Jeoffry! poor Jeoffry! the rat
has bit thy throat.

For I bless the name of the Lord Jesus that Jeoffry is better.

For the divine spirit comes about his body to sustain it in
compleat cat.

For his tongue is exceeding pure so that it has in purity what it
wants in musick.

For he is docile and can learn certain things.

For he can set up with gravity which is patience upon
approbation.

For he can fetch and carry, which is patience in employment.

For he can jump over a stick which is patience upon proof
positive.

For he can spraggle upon waggle at the word of command.

For he can jump from an eminence into his master's bosom.

For he can catch the cork and toss it again.
For he is hated by the hypocrite and miser.
For the former is afraid of detection.
For the latter refuses the charge.
For he camels his back to bear the first notion of business.
For he is good to think on, if a man would express himself neatly.
For he made a great figure in Egypt for his signal services.
For he killed the Icneumon-rat very pernicious by land.
For his ears are so acute that they sting again.
For from this proceeds the passing quickness of his attention.
For by stroaking of him I have found out electricity.
For I perceived God's light about him both wax and fire.
For the Electrical fire is the spiritual substance, which God sends
    from heaven to sustain the bodies both of man and beast.
For God has blessed him in the variety of his movements.
For, tho he cannot fly, he is an excellent clamberer.
For his motions upon the face of the earth are more than any other
    quadrupede.
For he can tread to all the measures upon the musick.
For he can swim for life.
For he can creep.

(Lines 697–770, Fragment B2)

CHRISTOPHER SMART

Not Waving but Drowning

Nobody heard him, the dead man,
But still he lay moaning:
I was much further out than you thought
And not waving but drowning.

Poor chap, he always loved larking
And now he's dead
It must have been too cold for him his heart gave way,
They said.

Oh, no no no, it was too cold always
(Still the dead one lay moaning)
I was much too far out all my life
And not waving but drowning.

STEVIE SMITH

The Old Man's Comforts

'You are old, Father William,' the young man cried,
   'The few locks that are left you are gray;
You are hale, Father William, a hearty old man;
   Now tell me the reason, I pray.'

'In the days of my youth,' Father William replied,
   'I remember'd that youth would fly fast,
And abused not my health and my vigour at first,
   That I never might need them at last.'

'You are old, Father William,' the young man cried,
   'And pleasures with youth pass away;
And yet you lament not the days that are gone;
   Now tell me the reason, I pray.'

'In the days of my youth,' Father William replied,
   'I remember'd that youth could not last;
I thought of the future; whatever I did,
   That I never might grieve for the past.'

'You are old, Father William,' the young man cried,
   'And life must be hast'ning away;
You are cheerful, and love to converse upon death;
   Now tell me the reason, I pray.'

'I am cheerful, young man,' Father William replied,
   'Let the cause thy attention engage;
In the days of my youth I remember'd my God,
   And He hath not forgotten my age.'

ROBERT SOUTHEY

The Inchcape Rock

No stir in the air, no stir in the sea,
The ship was still as she could be,
Her sails from heaven received no motion
Her keel was steady in the ocean.

Without either sign or sound of their shock
The waves flowed over the Inchcape Rock;
So little they rose, so little they fell,
They did not move the Inchcape Bell.

The worthy Abbot of Aberbrothok
Had placed that bell on the Inchcape Rock;
On a buoy in the storm it floated and swung,
And over the waves its warning rung.

When the rock was hid by the surges' swell,
The mariners heard the warning bell;
And then they knew the perilous rock,
And blest the Abbot of Aberbrothok.

The sun in heaven was shining gay,
All things were joyful on that day;
The sea-birds screamed as they wheel'd round,
And there was joyaunce in their sound.

The buoy of the Inchcape Bell was seen,
A darker speck on the ocean green;
Sir Ralph the Rover walk'd his deck,
And he fixed his eye on the darker speck.

He felt the cheering power of spring,
It made him whistle, it made him sing;
His heart was mirthful to excess,
But the Rover's mirth was wickedness.

His eye was on the Inchcape float;
Quoth he, 'My men, put out the boat,
And row me to the Inchcape Rock,
And I'll plague the Abbot of Aberbrothok.'

The boat is lowered, the boatmen row,
And to the Inchcape Rock they go ;
Sir Ralph bent over from the boat,
And he cut the bell from the Inchcape float.

Down sunk the bell with a gurgling sound –
The bubbles rose and burst around ;
Quoth Sir Ralph, 'The next who comes to the Rock
Won't bless the Abbot of Aberbrothok.'

Sir Ralph the Rover sailed away,
He scoured the seas for many a day ;
And now grown rich with plundered store,
He steers his course for Scotland's shore.

So thick a haze o'erspreads the sky
They cannot see the sun on high ;
The wind hath blown a gale all day,
At evening it hath died away.

On deck the Rover takes his stand,
So dark it is they see no land.
Quoth Sir Ralph, 'It will be lighter soon
For there is the dawn of the rising Moon.'

'Canst hear', said one, 'the breakers roar?
For methinks we should be near the shore.
Now where we are I cannot tell,
But I wish I could hear the Inchcape bell.'

They hear no sound – the swell is strong;
Though the wind hath fallen, they drift along.
Till the vessel strikes with a shivering shock, –
'Oh! heavens! it is the Inchcape Rock!'

Sir Ralph the Rover tore his hair ;
And curst himself in his despair ;
The waves rush in on every side.
The ship is sinking beneath the tide.

But even in his dying fear
One dreadful sound could the Rover hear,
A sound as if, with the Inchcape bell,
The Devil below was ringing his knell.

ROBERT SOUTHEY

Requiem

Under the wide and starry sky,
Dig the grave and let me lie.
Glad did I live and gladly die,
   And I laid me down with a will.

This be the verse you grave for me:
Here he lies where he longed to be;
Home is the sailor, home from sea,
   And the hunter home from the hill.

ROBERT LOUIS STEVENSON

Break, Break, Break

Break, break, break,
   On thy cold gray stones, O Sea!
And I would that my tongue could utter
   The thoughts that arise in me.

O well for the fisherman's boy,
   That he shouts with his sister at play!
O well for the sailor lad,
   That he sings in his boat on the bay!

And the stately ships go on
   To their haven under the hill;
But O for the touch of a vanished hand,
   And the sound of a voice that is still!

Break, break, break,
   At the foot of thy crags, O Sea!
But the tender grace of a day that is dead
   Will never come back to me.

ALFRED LORD TENNYSON

The Charge of the Light Brigade

Half a league, half a league,
Half a league onward,
All in the valley of Death
  Rode the six hundred.
'Forward, the Light Brigade!
Charge for the guns!' he said.
Into the valley of Death
  Rode the six hundred.

'Forward, the Light Brigade!'
Was there a man dismayed?
Not though the soldier knew
  Some one had blundered.
Theirs not to make reply,
Theirs not to reason why,
Theirs but to do and die.
Into the valley of Death
  Rode the six hundred.

Cannon to right of them,
Cannon to left of them,
Cannon in front of them
  Volleyed and thundered;
Stormed at with shot and shell,
Boldly they rode and well,
Into the jaws of Death,
Into the mouth of Hell
  Rode the six hundred.

Flashed all the sabres bare,
Flashed as they turned in air
Sabring the gunners there,
Charging an army, while
  All the world wondered:
Plunged in the battery-smoke
Right through the line they broke;
Cossack and Russian
Reeled from the sabre-stroke
  Shattered and sundered.
Then they rode back, but not,
  Not the six hundred.

Cannon to right of them,
Cannon to left of them,
Cannon behind them
  Volleyed and thundered;
Stormed at with shot and shell,
While horse and hero fell,
They that had fought so well
Came through the jaws of Death,
Back from the mouth of Hell,
All that was left of them,
  Left of six hundred.

When can their glory fade?
O the wild charge they made!
  All the world wondered.
Honour the charge they made!
Honour the Light Brigade,
  Noble six hundred!

———•◦•———

ALFRED, LORD TENNYSON

Crossing the Bar

Sunset and evening star,
  And one clear call for me!
And may there be no moaning of the bar,
  When I put out to sea,

But such a tide as moving seems asleep,
  Too full for sound and foam,
When that which drew from out the boundless
    deep
  Turns again home.

Twilight and evening bell,
  And after that the dark!
And may there be no sadness of farewell,
  When I embark;

For tho' from out our bourne of Time and Place
  The flood may bear me far,
I hope to see my Pilot face to face
  When I have crost the bar.

ALFRED, LORD TENNYSON

The Lady of Shalott

I

On either side the river lie
Long fields of barley and of rye,
That clothe the wold and meet the sky;
And thro' the field the road runs by
      To many-tower'd Camelot;
And up and down the people go,
Gazing where the lilies blow
Round an island there below,
      The island of Shalott.

Willows whiten, aspens quiver,
Little breezes dusk and shiver
Thro' the wave that runs for ever
By the island in the river
      Flowing down to Camelot.
Four gray walls, and four gray towers,
Overlook a space of flowers,
And the silent isle imbowers
      The Lady of Shalott.

By the margin, willow-veil'd,
Slide the heavy barges trail'd
By slow horses; and unhail'd
The shallop flitteth silken-sail'd
      Skimming down to Camelot:
But who hath seen her wave her hand?
Or at the casement seen her stand?
Or is she known in all the land,
      The Lady of Shalott?

Only reapers, reaping early
In among the bearded barley,
Hear a song that echoes cheerly
From the river winding clearly,
     Down to tower'd Camelot:
And by the moon the reaper weary,
Piling sheaves in uplands airy,
Listening, whispers ''Tis the fairy
     Lady of Shalott.'

II

There she weaves by night and day
A magic web with colours gay.
She has heard a whisper say,
A curse is on her if she stay
     To look down to Camelot.
She knows not what the curse may be,
And so she weaveth steadily,
And little other care hath she,
     The Lady of Shalott.

And moving thro' a mirror clear
That hangs before her all the year,
Shadows of the world appear.
There she sees the highway near
     Winding down to Camelot:
There the river eddy whirls,
And there the surly village-churls,
And the red cloaks of market girls,
     Pass onward from Shalott.

Sometimes a troop of damsels glad,
An abbot on an ambling pad,
Sometimes a curly shepherd-lad,
Or long-hair'd page in crimson clad,
     Goes by to tower'd Camelot;
And sometimes thro' the mirror blue
The knights come riding two and two:
She hath no loyal knight and true,
     The Lady of Shalott.

But in her web she still delights
To weave the mirror's magic sights,
For often thro' the silent nights
A funeral, with plumes and lights,
　　　And music, went to Camelot:
Or when the moon was overhead,
Came two young lovers lately wed;
'I am half sick of shadows,' said
　　　The Lady of Shalott.

III

A bow-shot from her bower-eaves,
He rode between the barley-sheaves,
The sun came dazzling thro' the leaves,
And flamed upon the brazen greaves
　　　Of bold Sir Lancelot.
A red-cross knight for ever kneel'd
To a lady in his shield,
That sparkled on the yellow field,
　　　Beside remote Shalott.

The gemmy bridle glitter'd free,
Like to some branch of stars we see
Hung in the golden Galaxy.
The bridle bells rang merrily
　　　As he rode down to Camelot:
And from his blazon'd baldric slung
A mighty silver bugle hung,
And as he rode his armour rung,
　　　Beside remote Shalott.

All in the blue unclouded weather
Thick-jewell'd shone the saddle-leather,
The helmet and the helmet-feather
Burn'd like one burning flame together,
　　　As he rode down to Camelot.
As often thro' the purple night,
Below the starry clusters bright,
Some bearded meteor, trailing light,
　　　Moves over still Shalott.

His broad clear brow in sunlight glow'd;
On burnish'd hooves his war-horse trode;
From underneath his helmet flow'd
His coal-black curls as on he rode,
  As he rode down to Camelot.
From the bank and from the river
He flash'd into the crystal mirror,
'Tirra lirra,' by the river
  Sang Sir Lancelot.

She left the web, she left the loom,
She made three paces thro' the room,
She saw the water-lily bloom,
She saw the helmet and the plume,
  She look'd down to Camelot.
Out flew the web and floated wide;
The mirror crack'd from side to side;
'The curse is come upon me,' cried
  The Lady of Shalott.

IV

In the stormy east-wind straining,
The pale yellow woods were waning,
The broad stream in his banks complaining,
Heavily the low sky raining
  Over tower'd Camelot;
Down she came and found a boat
Beneath a willow left afloat,
And round about the prow she wrote
  The Lady of Shalott.

And down the river's dim expanse –
Like some bold seër in a trance,
Seeing all his own mischance –
With a glassy countenance
  Did she look to Camelot.
And at the closing of the day
She loosed the chain, and down she lay;
The broad stream bore her far away,
  The Lady of Shalott.

Lying, robed in snowy white
That loosely flew to left and right –
The leaves upon her falling light –
Thro' the noises of the night
      She floated down to Camelot:
And as the boat-head wound along
The willowy hills and fields among,
They heard her singing her last song,
      The Lady of Shalott.

Heard a carol, mournful, holy,
Chanted loudly, chanted lowly,
Till her blood was frozen slowly,
And her eyes were darken'd wholly,
      Turn'd to tower'd Camelot.
For ere she reach'd upon the tide
The first house by the water-side,
Singing in her song she died,
      The Lady of Shalott.

Under tower and balcony,
By garden-wall and gallery,
A gleaming shape she floated by,
Dead-pale between the houses high,
      Silent into Camelot.
Out upon the wharfs they came,
Knight and burgher, lord and dame,
And round the prow they read her name,
      The Lady of Shalott.

Who is this? and what is here?
And in the lighted palace near
Died the sound of royal cheer;
And they cross'd themselves for fear,
      All the knights at Camelot:
But Lancelot mused a little space;
He said, 'She has a lovely face;
God in his mercy lend her grace,
      The Lady of Shalott.'

ALFRED, LORD TENNYSON

Do not go Gentle into that Good Night

Do not go gentle into that good night,
Old age should burn and rave at close of day;
Rage, rage against the dying of the light.

Though wise men at their end know dark is right,
Because their words had forked no lightning they
Do not go gentle into that good night.

Good men, the last wave by, crying how bright
Their frail deeds might have danced in a green bay,
Rage, rage against the dying of the light.

Wild men who caught and sang the sun in flight,
And learn, too late, they grieved it on its way,
Do not go gentle into that good night.

Grave men, near death, who see with blinding sight
Blind eyes could blaze like meteors and be gay,
Rage, rage against the dying of the light.

And you, my father, there on the sad height,
Curse, bless, me now with your fierce tears, I pray.
Do not go gentle into that good night.
Rage, rage against the dying of the light.

DYLAN THOMAS

Adlestrop

Yes. I remember Adlestrop –
The name, because one afternoon
Of heat the express-train drew up there
Unwontedly. It was late June.

The steam hissed. Someone cleared his throat.
No one left and no one came
On the bare platform. What I saw
Was Adlestrop – only the name

And willows, willow-herb, and grass,
And meadowsweet, and haycocks dry,
No whit less still and lonely fair
Than the high cloudlets in the sky.

And for that minute a blackbird sang
Close by, and round him, mistier,
Farther and farther, all the birds
Of Oxfordshire and Gloucestershire.

EDWARD THOMAS

Romance

When I was but thirteen or so
　I went into a golden land,
Chimborazo, Cotopaxi
　Took me by the hand.

My father died, my brother too,
　They passed like fleeting dreams.
I stood where Popocatapetl
　In the sunlight gleams.

I dimly heard the master's voice
　And boys far-off at play,
Chimborazo, Cotopaxi
　Had stolen me away.

I walked in a great golden dream
　To and fro from school –
Shining Popocatapetl
　The dusty streets did rule.

I walked home with a gold dark boy
　And never a word I'd say,
Chimborazo, Cotopaxi
　Had taken my speech away:

I gazed entranced upon his face
　Fairer than any flower –
O shining Popocatapetl
　It was thy magic hour:

The houses, people, traffic seemed
　Thin fading dreams by day,
Chimborazo, Cotopaxi
　They had stolen my soul away!

W. J. TURNER

O Captain! My Captain!

O Captain! my Captain! our fearful trip is done,
The ship has weather'd every rack, the prize we sought is won,
The port is near, the bells I hear, the people all exulting,
While follow eyes the steady keel, the vessel grim and daring;
    But O heart! heart! heart!
      O the bleeding drops of red,
        Where on the deck my Captain lies,
        Fallen cold and dead.

O Captain! my Captain! rise up and hear the bells;
Rise up – for you the flag is flung – for you the bugle trills,
For you bouquets and ribbon'd wreaths – for you the shores
    a-crowding,
For you they call, the swaying mass, their eager faces turning;
    Here Captain! dear father!
      This arm beneath your head!
      It is some dream that on the deck,
        You've fallen cold and dead.

My Captain does not answer, his lips are pale and still,
My father does not feel my arm, he has no pulse nor will,
The ship is anchor'd safe and sound, its voyage closed and done,
From fearful trip the victor ship comes in with object won:
    Exult O shores, and ring O bells!
      But I with mournful tread,
        Walk the deck my Captain lies,
        Fallen cold and dead.

WALT WHITMAN

Solitude

Laugh, and the world laughs with you,
   Weep, and you weep alone,
For sad old earth must borrow its mirth,
   But has trouble enough of its own.
Sing, and the hills will answer;
   Sigh, it is lost on the air,
The echoes bound to a joyful sound,
   But shrink from voicing care.

Rejoice, and men will seek you;
   Grieve, and they turn and go.
They want full measure of all your pleasure.
   But they do not need your woe.
Be glad, and your friends are many,
   Be sad, and you lose them all;
There are none to decline your nectared wine,
   But alone you must drink life's gall.

Feast, and your halls are crowded,
   Fast, and the world goes by.
Succeed and give – and it helps you live,
   But no man can help you die;
There is room in the halls of pleasure
   For a large and lordly train,
But one by one we must all file on
   Through the narrow aisles of pain.

ELLA WHEELER WILCOX

from *The Ballad of Reading Gaol*

Yet each man kills the thing he loves,
By each let this be heard,
Some do it with a bitter look,
Some with a flattering word.
The coward does it with a kiss,
The brave man with a sword!

OSCAR WILDE

The Burial of Sir John Moore after Corunna

Not a drum was heard, not a funeral note,
  As his corpse to the rampart we hurried;
Not a soldier discharged his farewell shot
  O'er the grave where our hero we buried.

We buried him darkly at dead of night,
  The sods with our bayonets turning,
By the struggling moonbeam's misty light
  And the lanthorn dimly burning.

No useless coffin enclosed his breast,
  Not in sheet or in shroud we wound him;
But he lay like a warrior taking his rest
  With his martial cloak around him.

Few and short were the prayers we said,
  And we spoke not a word of sorrow;
But we steadfastly gazed on the face that was dead,
  And we bitterly thought of the morrow.

We thought, as we hollowed his narrow bed
  And smoothed down his lonely pillow,
That the foe and the stranger would tread o'er his head,
  And we far away on the billow!

Lightly they'll talk of the spirit that's gone,
  And o'er his cold ashes upbraid him –
But little he'll reck, if they let him sleep on
  In the grave where a Briton has laid him.

But half of our heavy task was done
  When the clock struck the hour for retiring;
And we heard the distant and random gun
  That the foe was sullenly firing.

Slowly and sadly we laid him down,
    From the field of his fame fresh and gory;
We carved not a line, and we raised not a stone,
    But we left him alone with his glory.

———◆◆———

CHARLES WOLFE

I Wander'd Lonely as a Cloud

I wander'd lonely as a cloud
That floats on high o'er vales and hills,
When all at once I saw a crowd,
A host of golden daffodils,
Beside the lake, beneath the trees,
Fluttering and dancing in the breeze.

Continuous as the stars that shine
And twinkle on the milky way,
They stretch'd in never-ending line
Along the margin of a bay;
Ten thousand saw I at a glance
Tossing their heads in sprightly dance.

The waves beside them danced, but they
Out-did the sparkling waves in glee: –
A Poet could not but be gay
In such a jocund company!
I gazed – and gazed – but little thought
What wealth the show to me had brought;

For oft, when on my couch I lie
In vacant or in pensive mood,
They flash upon that inward eye
Which is the bliss of solitude;
And then my heart with pleasure fills,
And dances with the daffodils.

WILLIAM WORDSWORTH

My Heart Leaps Up

My heart leaps up when I behold
  A rainbow in the sky:
So was it when my life began,
So is it now I am a man,
So be it when I shall grow old
  Or let me die!
The Child is father of the Man:
And I could wish my days to be
Bound each to each by natural piety.

WILLIAM WORDSWORTH

The Solitary Reaper

Behold her, single in the field,
Yon solitary Highland Lass!
Reaping and singing by herself;
Stop here, or gently pass!
Alone she cuts and binds the grain,
And sings a melancholy strain;
O listen! for the vale profound
Is overflowing with the sound.

No nightingale did ever chaunt
More welcome notes to weary bands
Of travellers in some shady haunt,
Among Arabian sands:
A voice so thrilling ne'er was heard
In spring-time from the cuckoo-bird
Breaking the silence of the seas
Among the farthest Hebrides.

Will no one tell me what she sings?
Perhaps the plaintive numbers flow
For old, unhappy, far-off things,
And battles long ago:
Or is it some more humble lay,
Familiar matter of today?
Some natural sorrow, loss, or pain,
That has been, and may be again!

Whate'er the theme, the maiden sang
As if her song could have no ending;
I saw her singing at her work,
And o'er the sickle bending;
I listen'd, motionless and still;
And, as I mounted up the hill,
The music in my heart I bore,
Long after it was heard no more.

WILLIAM WORDSWORTH

Upon Westminster Bridge
Sept. 3, 1802

Earth has not anything to show more fair:
  Dull would he be of soul who could pass by
  A sight so touching in its majesty:
This City now doth, like a garment, wear
The beauty of the morning; silent, bare,
  Ships, towers, domes, theatres, and temples lie
  Open unto the fields, and to the sky;
All bright and glittering in the smokeless air.
Never did sun more beautifully steep
  In his first splendour, valley, rock, or hill;
Ne'er saw I, never felt, a calm so deep!
  The river glideth at his own sweet will:
Dear God! the very houses seem asleep;
  And all that mighty heart is lying still!

WILLIAM WORDSWORTH

The Lake Isle of Innisfree

I will arise and go now, and go to Innisfree,
And a small cabin build there, of clay and wattles made:
Nine bean-rows will I have there, a hive for the honey-bee,
And live alone in the bee-loud glade.

And I shall have some peace there, for peace comes dropping
  slow,
Dropping from the veils of the morning to where the cricket
  sings;
There midnight's all a glimmer, and noon a purple glow,
And evening full of the linnet's wings.

I will arise and go now, for always night and day
I hear lake water lapping with low sounds by the shore;
While I stand on the roadway, or on the pavements grey,
I hear it in the deep heart's core.

W. B. YEATS

Down by the Salley Gardens

Down by the salley gardens my love and I did meet;
She passed the salley gardens with little snow-white feet.
She bid me take love easy, as the leaves grow on the tree;
But I, being young and foolish, with her would not agree.

In a field by the river my love and I did stand,
And on my leaning shoulder she laid her snow-white hand.
She bid me take life easy, as the grass grows on the weirs;
But I was young and foolish, and now am full of tears.

W. B. YEATS

When You are Old

When you are old and grey and full of sleep,
And nodding by the fire, take down this book,
And slowly read, and dream of the soft look
Your eyes had once, and of their shadows deep;

How many loved your moments of glad grace,
And loved your beauty with love false or true,
But one man loved the pilgrim soul in you,
And loved the sorrows of your changing face;

And bending down beside the glowing bars,
Murmur, a little sadly, how Love fled
And paced upon the mountains overhead
And hid his face amid a crowd of stars.

W. B. YEATS

Index of First Lines

219